CONTENTS

INTRODUCTION   PAGE   8   CITIES: SMALL IS BEAUTIFUL   PAGE   74
UNITY IN DIVERSITY   PAGE   18   WHEN TRADITION IS A CHOICE   PAGE   124
THE ROOF OF EUROPE   PAGE   40   INDEX   PAGE   134

1 St. Gallen's historic center contains numerous gorgeous aristocratic residences dating back to between the 16th and 18th centuries; many have wooden façades painted in vibrant colors.

2-7 In this view of Lake Geneva, the Mont Blanc massif can be glimpsed in the background. The print, in the Geneva University Library, is the work of Carl Hackert (1740-1800).

3-6 The Bernese Alps have a special charm. The Jungfrau massif, center, and the Mönch and the Eiger on the left are trophies that climbers (and visitors) from around the world aspire to add to their collection.

WHITE STAR PUBLISHERS

Switzerland

PLACES AND HISTORY

Text by Moreno Bernasconi

Graphic design
Maria Cucchi

© 2006 White Star S.p.A.
Via Candido Sassone, 22/24
13100 Vercelli, Italy
www.whitestar.it

TRANSLATION:
AMY CHRISTINE EZRIN

ISBN 88-544-0138-2

REPRINTS:
1 2 3 4 5 6   10 09 08 07 06

Printed in China
Color separation Fotomec,
Turin

INTRODUCTION

9 top left A group of Swiss mountain people from the Valais region, in traditional garb, play the alpenhorn, a long wooden instrument whose base is rested against the ground.

9 top right During a festival, women from Appenzell Canton wear their traditional costume. In Inner Appenzell, women only gained the right to vote in 1990, following a decision of the Swiss Federal Court.

12-13 The Cathedral of Notre-Dame in Lausanne was consecrated in the 1276 by Pope Gregory X in the presence of Rudolph I of Hapsburg. It is the most beautiful Gothic construction in Switzerland. Since the Reformation it has been a Protestant church.

14-15 The view is idyllic: lush pastureland and peaks in the Klausen Pass area of Uri Canton. The canton, the custodian of the entrance to the St. Gotthard Pass, links the northern and southern regions of the Alps.

16-17 From the top of the Trugberg (12,904 feet), dawn breaks over the Mönch and Eiger.

8 The Matterhorn, like a giant crystal set into the chain of the Alps, straddling the Valais Canton and Italy, is one of Switzerland's most symbolic images.

8-9 The dial of a Girard-Perregaux chronometer is built by the expert hands of an artisan in La Chaux-de-Fonds, the cradle of the Swiss watch industry, the feather in the cap and emblem of Swiss "know-how."

S witzerland is like a mechanism formed of a series of different pieces in which the small wheels move the big ones, fitting into each other to produce slow but (at the end of the process) synchronized movement. The country has twenty-six cantons of very different sizes, with autonomous governments and parliaments, each largely independent from a financial point of view. Switzerland has four languages (Italian, French, German, and Romansch) and has two national creeds (Catholicism and Protestantism). A federal government of "seven wise men" elected by the Parliament represents all the main political forces of the country and linguistic regions, deliberating according to the principle of working in concert. There is no majority or opposition, no dissenting party, but rather Parliament was founded upon the practice of associating the opposition in government decisions, which works and has, in fact, greatly contributed to the nation's affluence. It is, in the end, the opinion of the people, who have been elected to the role of sovereign by direct democracy.

The Helvetian flag – a white cross on a red background – taken from the coat-of-arms of soldiers from the Canton of Schwyz who fought for Frederick II (Holy Roman Emperor, 1215-1250) emblematically indicates the country's geopolitical vocation. This alpine crossroads between north and south, between the east and west of Europe, has found itself in a position of defending its neutrality for centuries, a necessary stance to be able to uphold its role as guardian of the alpine passes, in the middle of the continent. The great European rivers and their tributaries originate at this crossroads: the Rhine, the Rhône, the Danube, and the Po. Despite reticence on the part of the majority of its people until now with respect to the European Union, geography has made of this region a deeply European nation.

Shut up in its impervious alpine prison, Switzerland was for centuries a very poor country. To survive, many of its sons had to enroll as mercenaries in the armies of the various European powers that were clashing on the fields of war, brother against brother. Later, many were forced to emigrate to other parts of Europe, the Americas, and Australia. Well-being came much later, and not only thanks to the hardworking Swiss citizens, but also to the skill and energy of generations of immigrants and refugees. They were industrial magnates and Huguenot bankers, then laborers, miners, masons, and artisans. Thereafter, not only men came to the country but also capital, which the Swiss copiously exploited in the *caveaux* of their financial institutions.

Swiss clichés are well known: the Matterhorn and the Jungfrau, the red Swiss Army pocketknife with all its gadgets, milk chocolate, watches, and of course, the banks. They are, whether they like it or not, the postcard photos for the land of Heidi. This book does not scorn clichés: it illustrates them, placing them within their geographical, historical, and cultural context. It seeks, however, to also reveal, from behind the façade, the hidden Switzerland, which is highly worth discovering. This is the intention of the volume you hold in your hands.

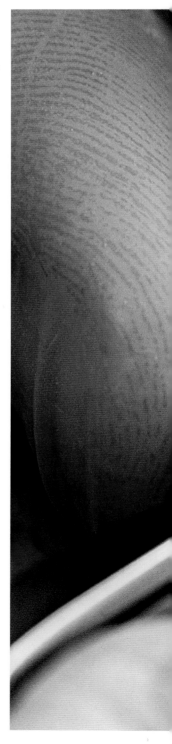

F r a n c e

Basle

Brugg —

Porrentruy

Aarau

St. Ursanne

Lenzburg

Aar River

Solothurn

La Chaux
de Fonds

Chasseral
(5,273 ft)

Bienne

Burgdorf

Bieler
See

Neuchâtel

Pilatus —
(6,985 ft)

La Brévine

Murten
See

Lake Neuchâtel

Berne

Sarnen —

Morat

Portalban

Aar

Yverdon

Thun

Fribourg

Interlaken

Aar

Sarine River

M o n t   R i s o u x

Romont

Lake
Thun

Grindelwald

Lake Joux

Le Moléson
(6,569 ft)

Gruyères

Eiger
(13,026 ft)

Morges

Lausanne

Mönch
(13,449 ft)

Lake Leman

Vevey

Jungfrau
(13,642 ft)

Nyon

Montreux

Crans/
Montana

Leukerbad

Aletschhorn
(13,764 ft)

Aigle

Rhône

Brig

Sion

Chandolin

Sempione

D i a b l e r e t s

Weisshorn
(14,781 ft)

Martigny

Dent Blanche
(14,295 ft)

Zermatt

G r a n d   C o m b i n
(14,154 ft)

The Matterhorn
(14,692 ft)

Mount Rosa
(15,204 ft)

Great St. Bernard

UNITY IN DIVERSITY

The human presence in Switzerland dates back to the Bronze Age, when primitive peoples built settlements on the shores of the lakes and rivers of the Swiss Plateau. During the Iron Age, the settlers moved to higher ground. Around the 4th century B.C., economic development began with the arrival of Celts, including the Helvetians; these tribes moved into the territories between Lake Constance, the Rhine River, the Jura Mountains, and Lake Geneva. The Celts introduced the art of working with precious metals and they minted coins. South of the Alps and in the present-day Grisons, Rhaetians and Lepontians settled. The Helvetians built some 400 villages and 12 cities, serving a total of 400,000 inhabitants (as recorded by Julius Caesar, who feared them). In 58 B.C. they burned their villages and moved toward Gaul. Caesar's troops stopped them at Bibracte (near Autun, in France) and forced them to turn back. From then on, the Helvetians (who in 107 B.C. had humiliatingly defeated the Romans at Agen) submitted to the rule of Rome. Rome founded colonies of veterans at Augusta Raurica (Augst) and at Julia Equestris (Nyon, on the shores of Lake Geneva). At Vindonissa (Windisch, in Aargau) Roman generals stationed a garrison, and Aventicum (Avenches, near Fribourg) became the capital of Helvetia. The construction of Aosta and the Romanization of Celtic Octodurus (Martigny) made it possible to monitor the Great St. Bernard Pass and the Rhône Valley, while the Rhaetian passes allowed for links between the capital of the Empire and the Rhine Valley. A period of peace and relative prosperity reigned until the end of the 3rd century B.C., when the Germanic tribes began their invasions, with the Alemanni devastating the east and the milder Burgundians occupying the west. This division created a linguistic and cultural watershed that still remains in place: the east has maintained its Germanic culture while the west adopted the Christian religion and a Romance language. The Alemanni were pagans and savages, and the autochthonous population sought refuge in the Alps. The Germanization ended up overtaking a vast area, from Lake Constance to the Alps, as far as the River Sarine, which still separates French from German Switzerland. On the other side of the Alps, the Rhaetian valleys maintained their Latin-based language, Romansch, and modern-day Ticino stayed within the Italic sphere, in the Lombard kingdom. The Alemanni slowly converted to Christianity thanks to the efforts of the monks of St. Columba and St. Gallen and the French Merovingian and Carolingian kings.

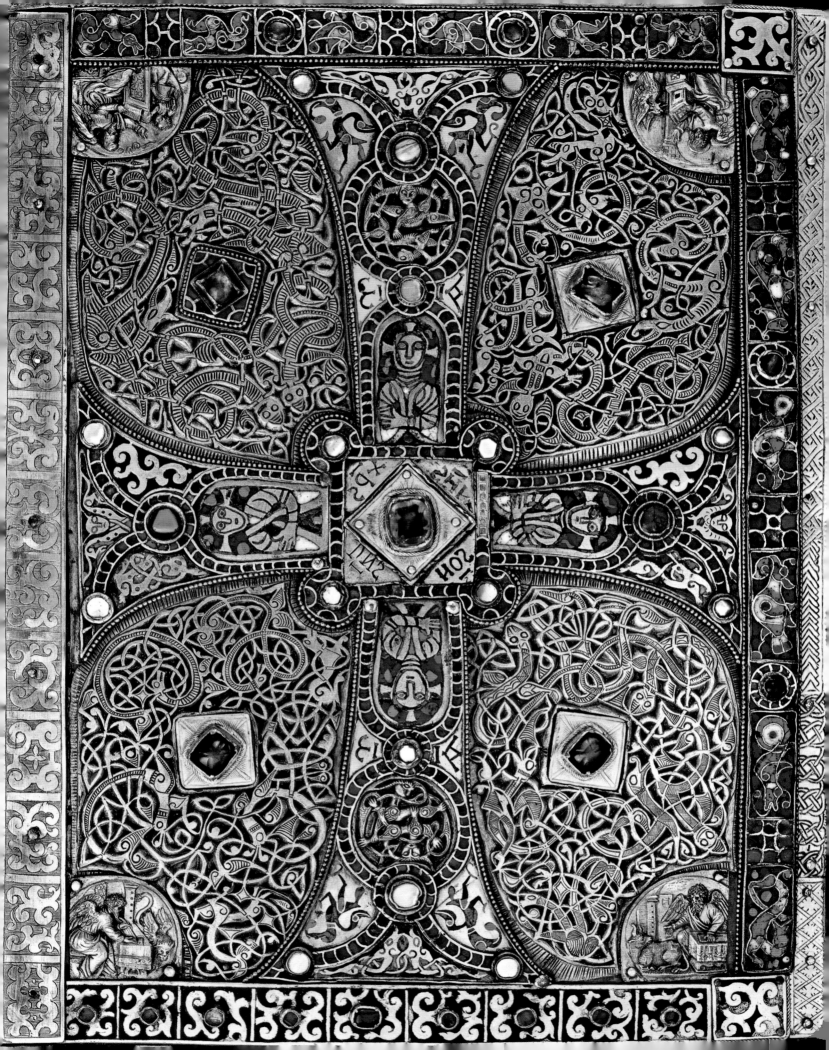

In Helvetian lands, the spread of Christianity did not blur the division between the Latin and Germanic cultures: when, in the 9th century, Charlemagne's Empire became divided, the border was once again set to pass vertically through the middle of Switzerland. In the late 12th century, Switzerland was an integral part of the Holy Roman Empire, under the crown of which Germany, Italy, Burgundy, Savoy, and Provence were united. Some families expanded their power through the foundation of cities and their control of key points in the Empire. In the Swiss territory, the Savoy family dominated the western Alps from the Great St. Bernard Pass to Saint Maurice, from Chillon as far as Vaud. The Hapsburgs, in addition to holding lands in Alsace, controlled a good part of the territory of Aargau. The Zähringen dynasty founded the cities of Bern, Fribourg, and Morat, but then died out. The Savoys, and above all the Hapsburgs, took advantage of this fact and even confiscated the holdings of the Kyburgs to go on to dominate a vast portion of the territory of central and eastern Switzerland.

By the 13th century, Switzerland already possessed a dense network of cities. Besides those cities and towns already mentioned, St. Gallen, Zürich, Basel, Solothurn, and Lucerne obtained imperial privileges and wide-ranging autonomy. In the rural zones, united communities governed "democratically" according to the principles of free assembly. Until the 12th century, crossing the Alps took place via the Great St. Bernard, Lukmanier, and Splügen passes. At the be-

ginning of the 13th century, the inhabitants of the regions in Uri made the St. Gotthard Pass feasible, thus initiating a heavy flow of goods and pilgrims across the central Alps.

During the first half of the 13th century, the importance of the St. Gotthard Pass induced the Holy Roman Emperor, Frederick II of Hohenstaufen, to sign two treaties, first with Uri and then with Schwyz, promising protection that would liberate these rural communities from obligations to the Hapsburgs. This privileged situation did not last for very long. Once elected to the German throne in 1273, Rudolf of Hapsburg became emperor *ipso facto*, and the people of Uri and Schwyz saw their adversaries turn into their sovereigns. Rudolf sent his own officials (bailiffs) into central Switzerland, individuals of inferior lineage who nonetheless had the authority to collect taxes, levy tolls on the St. Gotthard Pass, and enforce the law. This situation finally pushed the people of central Switzerland (the so-called Waldstätten, or the "forest cantons") to build alliances to safeguard their autonomy and privileges. Just two weeks after the death of Rudolf on 1 August 1291, fearing they would lose what little freedom they had managed to keep under him, the Waldstätten vowed reciprocal aid and defense. The pact was of unlimited duration, had the purpose of safeguarding internal peace, and provided for mutual defensive and offensive assistance against anyone who might threaten a member of the league. The league could count on the support of Zürich, a city that enjoyed imperial

privileges. The central principle of the pact ratifying the birth of the Helvetic Confederation (August 1 is now a national holiday) was the rejection of foreign judges. The Waldstätten did not deny the authority of the king, however they demanded the right to be judged by their peers and above all by inhabitants of their towns, hence by judges who knew the customs of the place. A legendary tradition (consecrated by Schiller and Rossini) sees the Swiss national hero in William Tell. Intolerant of the arrogance of Rudolf's officials, he dared to challenge Gessler, the "cruel bailiff," in the central square of Altdorf. Forced by the minor officer to shoot an apple balanced his son's head with an arrow, Tell hit the target but not without having first prepared a second arrow

intended for Gessler in the event he missed his first shot. Condemned to prison, he made a daring escape and then ambushed and killed the officer. As for the vow of reciprocal assistance, legend has it that it was solemnly sworn on the Rütli Meadow, on the shores of the Lake of the Four Cantons, by Werner Stauffacher (from Uri), Walter Fürst (from Schwyz), and Arnold von Melchtal (from Unterwalden). The history of the old Helvetic Confederation (1291-1798) is a series of pacts of reciprocal aid between rural towns and cities to uphold local autonomy, starting with that between Uri, Schwyz, and Unterwalden (renewed in 1315) to the League of the Thirteen Cantons (1513), which lasted until the Helvetian Republic of 1798. Dependence on

the Empire, which guaranteed the Confederates (the *Eidgenossen*, or "those bound by the vow") vast autonomy, and the centuries-old conflict with the Hapsburgs characterized the medieval era. The Confederates defeated the Hapsburgs at Morgarten (1315); Sempach (1386), where Duke Leopold III of Austria lost his life; and Näfels (1388). At the crowning of Albert II of Hapsburg (1438), even Aargau – where the house of Austria had solid roots – was by then an integral part of the Helvetian federal treaty, though only as a dependent territory. After the emancipation of Thurgau (1460), the Confederates achieved the finalization of a perpetual peace treaty with Austria that recognized their regions' autonomy within the Empire.

22 top left A Swiss soldier, in his traditional uniform, is portrayed in this 1572 print by Jean Sluperius.

22-23 In the battle of Marignano, fought near Pavia, on September 13 and 14, 1515, the troops of Francis I of France defeated the Swiss, an event that marked the end of the Helvetic Confederation's expansionistic aims.

In the 15th century, thanks to military successes against the meddling Austrians (and to a convergence of interests with the Empire), the Confederates expanded their territory. Uri and Obwald, which controlled the St. Gotthard Pass, the commercial gateway to Italy, occupied territory south of the Alps (the Leventina) belonging to the duke of Milan (whom they defeated at the Battle of Giornico in 1478). Bern expanded west toward Fribourg and Vaud; Zürich to the northeast toward Thurgau and Schaffhausen. At the end of the century, these towns and Zürich responded to Bern's call to arms and declared war against Charles the Bold, duke of Burgundy, whom they defeated at Grandson and Morat (in 1476) and at Nancy (1477), going on to initiate a policy of southward expansion.

The splitting up of the war booty, heavy external pressure, and disagreement between rural and city cantons brought about serious internal division, which was overcome in 1481 with the Stans Convention, thanks to the charismatic intervention of the hermit Nicholas of Flue. Fribourg and Solothurn at the heart of the discord, were admitted into the Confederation, and a few years Basel, Schaffhausen, and Appenzell (in 1513) were also admitted.

The interests of the Empire and the France (in addition to those of the Papacy) were, in the meantime, concentrated on Italy, particularly on Milan. Without the help of the Confederates, who had occupied Bellinzona, Riviera and Blenio, Locarno and Vallemaggia, Lugano, and Mendrisio and had contributed to the installation of Maximilian, the son of Ludovic "the Moor" Sforza, on the throne of Milan as per the Emperor's wish, it was impossible for the two big contenders to extend their power into Italy. Francis I of France was unable to convince all the Swiss to join his side, but he acquired (by buying them off) the non-belligerence of the western cantons and the services of many mercenaries. This move succeeded in halving the number of Swiss troops siding against the French on the field at Marignano on September 13, 1515, making it possible for Francis I to win a battle that would have a decisive outcome for the Confederates. The treaty calling for perpetual peace signed with the French after the victory at Marignano (and the cooperation of the mercenary conscripts) gave rise to a period of intense and uninterrupted collaboration between the Swiss and their powerful neighbor, an alliance that would last until the installation by force, on the part of the French in 1798, of the Helvetian Republic. Though they managed to hold on to the Ticino commons (i.e., dependent territories, administered by one or more cantons) south of the Alps, from that moment on, the Swiss abandoned all expansionistic wishful thinking.

Above all, internal divisions due to disagreements between cities and country towns and the devastating consequences of the heavy draft of Swiss soldiers were responsible for the military weakening of the Confederation of the Thirteen Cantons. The creation of the first confederate state governing body, the so-called Diet – which consisted of two representatives from each canton, met regularly, and whose members voted on the basis of instructions from their districts – was, nonetheless, unable to heal these divisions. The binding agreements that kept the old Confederation together were legal bonds forming the basis for pacts of reciprocal alliance and an organization of power not based on force but on the exercise of recognized duties and rights. The authorities' right

to hold the draft and to collect taxes was balanced by those of their subjects, who enjoyed ample autonomy at the community level. In the cities, the aristocracy governed, and in the countryside, the so-called *Landsgemeinde*. This institution, which was formed in the 14th century in the rural regions alongside the expansion of the urban guilds, was an assembly of all members of the community who enjoyed political rights, in which members voted by raising their hand. This political culture acted as the glue binding a confederation whose unity the Protestant Reformation had strongly compromised.

23 bottom St. Nicholas of Flue (portrayed here in a 17th-century painting), who left his family to withdraw to the hermitage of the Ranft, near Stans, was among the first to praise the merits of Swiss neutrality, the true antidote to the attempts of foreign powers to divide the Swiss into factions.

In Switzerland the humanistic movement of the Protestant Reformation contributed to the growth of a federal conscience and to the study of biblical texts and the writings of the Church Fathers. It was also the cultural stew in which the roots of the Swiss Protestant movement were blended into the mix. Ulrich Zwingli, who became curator of the Grossmünster in Zürich in 1518 and who was the Protestant movement's most important spokesman, explained the New Testament to his disciples through the study of ancient texts. However, his positions were so radical as to worry Erasmus and give rise to clear differences of opinion with Martin Luther himself. In efforts that he claimed were aimed at renewing evangelical purity, he ended up abolishing the Eucharist, stripping the churches of all ornament, disbanding the monasteries, and confiscating the Church's assets. Zürich's upper class saw in the new religion the possibility to consolidate their own power, and in 1525, the Council of Zürich voted to adhere to Zwingli's theories and immediately confiscated land and the monasteries' rights to tithes and property in the city and outside its walls. Thereafter, the movement also overtook Bern (1528), Basel (1529), and then Schaffhausen and St. Gallen, Solothurn, and Fribourg. These last two cities later returned to the Catholic camp. The reforms created a deep split. There were not only religious matters at stake but significant political and economic interests: the rural cantons saw a movement in the Reformation that, empowering the cities to the detriment of the countryside, would present a threat to

their independence. The issue of the commons, managed alternately by the Catholic and Protestant cantons, aggravated the situation. The Protestants were using them to proselytize while the Catholics fought them calling them heretics. It ended in a call to arms (the wars of Kappel in 1529 and 1531) and the Protestants were defeated. Zwingli was killed and the majority of the commons returned to the Catholic side. From then on, religious divisions were final. At that time, the map of the country looked as follows: the original cantons of Uri, Schwyz, Unterwalden, plus Lucerne, Zug, and Fribourg, as well as the Italian commons are Catholic; Zürich, Bern, Basel, and Schaffhausen are Protestant. The two religions can both be freely observed in the cantons of Glarus and Appenzell (both would later be divided into two half-cantons). At first, western Switzerland was not affected by the Reformation. Bern's later conquest of Vaud (1536) and Calvin's proselytizing in Geneva opened the door to the Reformation. The Grisons were divided between the Catholic and Protestant regions. Thus from the Reformation on, two Christian churches (split up according to the principle of *cuius regio, eius religio*, "whose the region is, his the religion") existed in Switzerland. They put up with each other, but had to deal with internal tribulations. The Swiss Protestants had to carve out their own place with respect to the Lutherans and Anabaptists, not to mention a place within the reformed churches of Europe, and this occurred only in 1566, the date of the declaration of the Second Helvetic Confession of Faith, in which Zwingli's successor, Heinrich Bullinger, spelled out the Protestant creed. The Catholics, after the Council of Trent (1545-1563), faced a difficult internal reform, pushed forward by figures such as Carlo Borromeo. The Jesuits advised the élite; the Capuchins served the common folk.

The religious wars raging across Europe worsened internal divisions. The many creeds available continued to be ever more indicative of the existence of two Confederations practicing different policies: that of the Catholic cantons, which first asked Austria and then Spain for aid, and that of the Protestant cantons, which looked to France (until the Calvinist Huguenots started to be persecuted). The equilibrium (with the Catholic cantons

being in the majority, but the four large Protestant cities having larger military forces at their disposal) and the accord regarding mercenary conscription signed with France in 1515 prevented civil war from dissolving the Confederation. The cantons could refuse to send their soldiers in the event of war: it was in the interests of Louis XIII of France to encourage peace among the cantons. He did so. During the Thirty Years' War (1618-1648), the same scenario repeated itself: the contending parties asked the Swiss for aid, who nonetheless preferred to remain neutral. Only the Grisons – where the passes were of strategic importance to Spain and France – was unable to avoid becoming involved. The canton was forced to pay a high price in blood, as the dramatic story of Jörg Jenatsch well illustrates. Nevertheless, the Swiss had understood that without their own army, it would have been difficult for the nation to maintain neutrality. The Defense Charter of Wil (1647) instituted military training for all males, the beginning of what would become armed neutrality. The next year, the Treaty of Westphalia, which ended the Thirty Years' War, recognized the independence of the Confederation on an international level.

26 top left During the time of Louis XIV (1643-1715), the Swiss Confederation was composed of thirteen cantons. Their representatives were received at Versailles on 11 November 1663. This painting, in the Palace of Versailles, is from 1664.

*26 top right
Geneva's most
illustrious sons
include Jean-Jacques
Rousseau, the father
of the modern "social
contract" and
author of universally
known literary
works.*

*26-27 The ideas
of the French
Revolution were*

*contagious to the souls
of many in Geneva;
this watercolor by
Christian Geissler
portrays the return of
the General Council
on 10 February 1789.
Napoleon's French
troops invaded
Switzerland in 1789,
declaring the Helvetic
Republic, based on
the French model,
in 1798.*

*27 top right In the
18th and 19th
centuries, several
Swiss cities – among
them Geneva, Basel,
and Zürich –
experienced
extraordinary
advances in the
sciences thanks to
important researchers
like Giovanni
Bernoulli and
Leonhard Euler.*

The Reformation had important economic consequences. It consolidated the power of the aristocracy in the cities and made it possible for the Protestant cantons to benefit from an entrepreneurial class that had had to flee Holland, Italy, and France because of religious persecution (especially after France revoked the pro-Protestant Edict of Nantes in 1685). They were merchants and owners of companies expert at working wool and silk, watchmaking, or were in banking. Industries developed at an extraordinary rate, giving work even to the rural regions surrounding the cities. The 17th and 18th centuries saw wealth-producing, booming manufacturing businesses take root, above all in the Protestant cantons. The wealthy aristocrats invested their capital in the countryside, increasing production from the land. Even in the mountain regions and in central Switzerland, livestock raising flourished and commercial activity was lucrative. Furthermore, military service abroad had made quite a few officers rich.

France was by now the primary European power and reinforced its influence over Switzerland. In 1633, Louis XIII renewed the treaty of alliance treaty between France and the Confederate cantons, ratifying the mercenary draft first agreed to in 1515. In the exchange, Switzerland obtained territorial recognition and a series of economic and political privileges, almost as if it were a French protectorate. Having remained Catholic, Solothurn was chosen by Louis XIII as the headquarters of France's ambassadors to the Diet of the Swiss Cantons. French influence also coincided with the spread of absolutist ideas in Switzerland. Above all in the cities, oligarchic and aristocratic management of power took root. A tight group of upper-class families controlled the city guilds and kept the trades and more lucrative businesses under their control; they also kept politics and public offices within a closed circle.

By the 17th century, the city aristocracies had put an authoritarian type of political control into place: they limited and finally abolished consideration of public opinion, and entire rural communities, from which all autonomy had been withdrawn, were reduced to being their subjects. In truth, even in the countryside, though they had not been able to abolish the Landsgemeinde assemblies, a few patrician families dominated the scene, harshly limiting any democratic participation.

Tensions between the cities and farmers, who were burdened by taxes and defrauded of their ancient rights, came to a head in the "farmers' war" of 1653 and in those of Villmergen in 1656 and 1712. The latter two conflicts, which set the rural Catholic cantons and the urban Protestant cantons against each other in a violent clash, took on a prominently religious nature. The Protestants' clear victories of Zürich and Bern in 1712, followed by the treaty of Aarau, altered the balance of power within the Confederation in their favor.

In the 18th century, French influence also opened Switzerland to literature and rationalist ideas. While the country was making no progress in the political and social spheres, new cultural ideas were being widespread by the self-styled Swiss Society. Mathematicians like Bernoulli and Euler, philosophers like Rousseau, and pedagogues like Pestalozzi became intellectual forces recognized throughout Europe.

*27 bottom right The
research and works of
Leonhard Euler, from
Basel, were the basis
of modern algebra.*

At the beginning of 1798, the French army burst into Lausanne and continued its advance, occupying a Switzerland that – as custodian of the alpine passes – was a strategic factor if troops had to move from Paris to Milan. The Vaud region, under the control of Bern, took advantage of the situation to proclaim the Lemanic Republic. The road to freedom also opened up for the citizens of the Italian commons. Zürich and Schaffhausen granted equal rights to all their citizens. When heralding the end of the aristocracy's privileges, French bayonets encountered heavy resistance only in central Switzerland and in Bern, which city they stormed, obtaining a fortune in war booty. Swiss territory was, nonetheless, plundered, and the population was required to pay heavy tributes.

Napoleon's troops imposed severely centralized rule on Switzerland, based on the French model, which removed every sovereign right from the cantons and reduced them to simple districts. In the place of the Diet, Napoleon established a directorate of five members that nominated ministers and governors to the cantons, districts, and towns. The big electors, designated by primary assemblies, had to elect the High Council entrusted to exercise legislative power. In the five years it lasted, the Helvetic Republic abolished feudal privileges, repealed tithes and land censuses, and created plans to reform education, money-minting, and unify the postal service; however, it also whetted the conflict between federalists (advocates of reinstituting cantonal sovereignty) and centralists (supporters of the new state model).

28-29 At Zürich in 1799, the French general Massena defeated Suvorov, the leader of the Austrian-Russian army, which had crossed the Alps via the St. Gotthard Pass. This painting by François Bouchot is in the Museum of the Palace of Versailles.

28 top The Austrian-Russian army built a bridge over the Rhine on December 21 and 22, 1813, to allow for the passage of their troops.

28 bottom In December 1813, Switzerland let Austrian-Russian troops cross the Rhine at Basel to invade neighboring France.

Thus, when the European powers declared war on Napoleon Bonaparte's France, Switzerland maintained a position of neutrality relative to its neighbor, with whom it had always had strong ties. Even when, in 1797, French troops occupied the Jura region belonging to the bishopric of Basel, the city's High Council did not react negatively.

Following the invitation of Peter Ochs, a stalwart supporter of the new revolutionary ideas, city authorities accorded political rights and freedom to their subjects.

Coups d'état followed one after the other at an escalating rate, launching the country into a dramatic civil war. The increasingly chaotic situation pushed Napoleon himself to put an end to the experiment of the Helvetian Republic and to reestablish, in 1803 with a solemn "Act of Mediation," a system of a federal nature ("Nature has made your state federal, to seek to overturn that would not be the act of a wise man"). Napoleon's Act of Mediation returned to the cantons the status of independent statehood and sanctioned the birth of six new ones: Vaud (by now liberated from Bern), the ancient territories subject to Ticino, Aargau and Thurgau, as well as those allied with the Grisons and St. Gallen. Furthermore, he added to the cantonal constitutions a fundamental 19-member charter that, from that moment on, would be called the Helvetic Confederation.

However, Napoleon's intervention reduced Switzerland to a condition of vassalage to France; the Swiss had had guarantee a large number of conscripts for service in the French army, an obligation that could never be fully honored and that several times pushed the Emperor to threaten pure and simple annexation. On the other hand, Napoleon's Cisalpine troops had already occupied Ticino Canton when they were recalled to attend to other military obligations, as his star was by now no longer rising.

The defeat of Napoleon banished the specter of annexation but not that of civil war. However, in 1814, thanks to the direct intervention of Czar Alexander of Russia, the old cantons were forced to acknowledge the independence of the new ones.

Switzerland had to wait for the Congress of Vienna (1815) to recover its independence and recognition of an armed neutrality. The borders were redrawn in Vienna. Valais, Neuchâtel, and Geneva, old allied territories belonging to France, formed three new cantons. The Bernese representatives at the congress also managed to obtain compensation for the lands of Vaud and Aargau lost during the Napoleonic period. A part of the Jura (Catholic and French-speaking) belonging to the Episcopal principality was given to the Bern Canton (Protestant with a German-speaking majority). Switzerland was not able, however, to regain the Valtellina, in which Austria was particularly interested.

From an economic point of view, given that peace had returned to Europe, the new federal pact of 1815 favored the development of a country that had lived through many years of extreme poverty. Large investments were made in highways, bridges, and communications, and with improvements in transportation, Swiss industries experienced a period of great growth. Agricultural production went through an upswing and even the countryside grew rich. A budding tourism industry attracted many travelers to this country endowed with beautiful natural settings, but until then little known. The basis for the long-term development of the hotel, guesthouse and tourism industries was created. However, no political development accompanied the economic expansion. The restoration of the Ancien Régime soon revealed itself to be a lid under which boiled a pot of explosive conflicts. The progressive cantons offered refuge to French, German and other revolutionaries, including the Russian anarchist Bakunin and the Italian independence leaders Mazzini and Carlo Cattaneo; collectively these refugees had a notable influence on Swiss political life. The reaction of the Holy Alliance (Russia, Prussia, and Austria) and the threat of invasion grew weighty enough at that point to force the cantonal authorities to intervene against the revolutionaries sheltered in Switzerland. However, large circles of intellectuals and politicians mobilized to support them, thus initiating the clash between liberals and conservatives.

After 1830 (the year of the revolutionary movement in Paris), thanks to the numerous civil associations that had developed during the previous years, many popular demonstrations were held that brought about the expansion of democratic rights. From 1839 to 1848, the political fight heated up, provoking coups d'état and open civil war. In 1839, radical liberals overthrew the conservative government of Ticino Canton while they were thrown out of that in Zürich. In 1841, the radical liberal government of Aargau closed down eight monasteries. In 1844, the civil war in the Valais resulted in the victory of the conservatives, and the government of Lucerne recalled the previously expelled Jesuits. In 1845, the radical liberals overthrew the moderate liberals in Geneva, and in Lucerne the leader of the liberals was condemned to death but managed to escape, whereas the leader of the conservatives was assassinated. In December, under strict secrecy, the separatist league of the conservative cantons (the so-called Sonderbund, consisting of the Catholic cantons of Uri, Schwyz, Unterwalden, Zug, Fribourg, and Valais) was founded with the intention of defending the cantons' rights and territories. The civil war worsened, in part because the separatist league had asked conservative foreign powers for aid. In July 1847, the federal Diet granted the radical liberals' request for the dissolution of the separatist league. Faced with the Catholic cantons' refusal to cooperate, in November, the Diet ordered the league's dissolution. General Dufour, a man of moderate beliefs, led the military campaign, managing to prevent it from degenerating. Dufour defeated the Sonderbund's troops, but the dead numbered no more than about 100 and the wounded no more than about 500. After only three weeks, on November 24, 1847, the civil

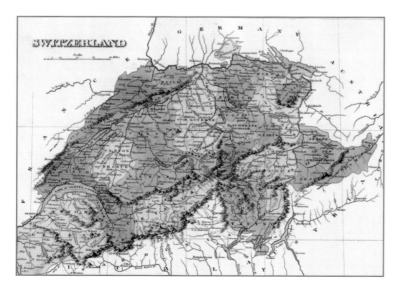

war had ended with the defeat of the Sonderbund, and when Austria, Prussia, and France offered to mediate, the radicals were able to pronounce the offer unneeded. Strengthened by their victory, the radical liberals demanded of the defeated that the federal pact of 1815 be revised and that the requirement for unanimous decisions be abandoned in favor of majority decisions by member states. The new federal constitution was accepted by the vote of 1848 and entered into effect immediately. The parliament was set up based on the American model: two legislative chambers endowed with the same powers, the National Council (representative of the people) and the Council of the States or Chamber of the Cantons (with 44 members, two representatives from each canton, regardless of its size). Bern was chosen to be the capital and headquarters of the parliament, the federal government, and the administration. Lausanne became the seat of the federal court. As early as 1840, the Diet – upon the advice that Dufour had given in 1815 – decided to adopt a single national flag. The Swiss flag, with the white cross on a red background, is derived from that which Emperor Frederick II had given to his faithful soldiers from Schwyz in the 13th century.

32 top In 1912, in only four months, the metal structure covering the tracks of the Lausanne station was built.

32 bottom left The St. Gotthard Tunnel was completed in 1880. About 2000 people were involved in its construction.

32 bottom right and 33 The poster celebrates the inauguration of the Simplon Tunnel in 1906. The photograph portraying a group of workers in front of the tunnel is from 1899.

The sensible political balance preserved by the new federal state, based predominantly on liberalism and industrial development, whose basic principles had been drafted at the beginning of the 19th century, gave crucial momentum during the in the second half of the century to the creation of vast infrastructures. Bridges, roadways, and railways could be built in part thanks to the birth of large banking (Crédit Suisse) and insurance (Rentenanstalt) institutions. In order to give new impetus to the scientific studies that had long flourished in Switzerland, the Confederation chose to maintain the universities already established in several cantons, and to add to them a new national Polytechnic Institute, which opened in 1854.

Thanks to significant financial support, the Federal Polytechnic Institute of Zürich became a scientific school of great international prestige, a driving force in techno-

logical research and progress, of which Swiss industries could make practical use. Already the cradle of an extraordinary expansion in manufacturing in the 17th century, at the end of the 19th century Switzerland had acquired an enviable position on the international industrial scene. The textile industry had branches in Zürich, Appenzell, Basel, and St. Gallen, the traditional home of lace-making.

The Jura and Neuchâtel specialized in watchmaking. The machine industry, in a country lacking in primary materials, was oriented above all toward precision engineering. The chemical industry appeared and thereafter grew strong roots in the Basel area, taking advantage of the country's large hydro-electric resources.

If the movement and export of goods was to flourish, then efficient railway connections were vital. The network developed rapidly thanks above all to extremely aggres-

sive private initiative, a superiority not necessarily in the public's immediate interest and one that provoked heated debate in the parliament and in public opinion. Arguments reached their peak when the location of a tunnel through the Alps had to be decided: Simplon, St. Gotthard, or Splügen? The "quarrels" were resolved in favor of St. Gotthard because of its central position and through the political and financial support of Bismarck's Germany and the new kingdom of Italy. Sympathetic to the liberal ideas of the Helvetic Confederation, Rome lent its ear to the skillful Swiss plenipotentiary ambassador, Giovan Battista Pioda. The railway tunnel was finished in just ten years, between 1872 and 1882. In 1906, the Simplon tunnel was completed. The Helvetic Confederation could by now count on a vast railroad network that improved internal transportation and favored exportation and the tourism industry.

INAUGURATION DU TUNNEL DU SIMPLON
EXPOSITION INTERNATIONALE
MILAN = 1906
AVRIL = NOVEMBRE

C. RICORDI & C. MILAN

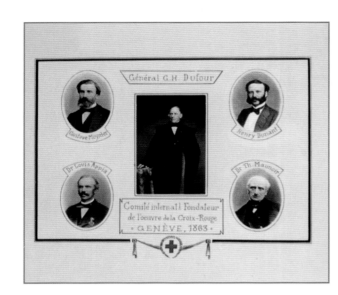

34 top left The first International Committee of the Red Cross was constituted in Geneva in 1863.

34 top right Geneva is the international headquarters of the Convention of the same name, the foundation of international human rights, drafted there in 1864 and expanded in 1899 and 1929.

At the same pace as industrial development, workers' rights in Switzerland also improved. The Constitution of 1848 was incomplete from the standpoint of social guarantees: there were no limits to the length of the workday and woman and children were being exploited in an abusive and intolerable way, particularly in the textile industry. The Constitution of 1874 established federal rules that prevented employers from moving factories to take advantage of lesser restrictions in some of the cantons. In 1877, a law regulating factory labor was approved. At the beginning of the 20th century, federal assistance in case of illness was encouraged, and businesses were required to insure their employees in case of accident.

The worker's movement – rather moderate at the time of the Grütli Patriotic and Social Society – continued organizing. Around 1870, the Swiss Labor Federation and the socialist party were born, the latter having, with the passage of time, radicalized its political agenda, taking openly anti-military positions and supporting the struggle of the lower classes.

In the meantime, under the influence of European events, the Helvetic Confederation decided to create a federal army able to defend the country's neutrality (1870). A few years earlier, in 1863, Henry Dunant of Geneva – a first-hand witness of the atrocious suffering of soldiers in the field at the battle of Solferino – had founded the International Red Cross, thus giving new meaning to Swiss neutrality and initiating a humanitarian tradition that would grow deep roots. Geneva would be the headquarters of the institution and its emblem the Swiss flag, but with the cross in red and the background white.

In order to generally strengthen direct democracy and popular rights, in 1874 the people and cantons accepted a revision of the federal constitution that sanctioned the extension of popular rights. Early on, the institution of the facultative referendum on laws voted in by Parliament was introduced. In 1891, the right to amend the constitution was approved, on the basis of which the people can modify an existing article or create new ones. To be adopted, a constitutional amendment had to (and still has to) be approved not only by the majority of the people but also by that of the cantons. The Constitution of 1874 also contained articles of a clearly anti-clerical nature that incited harsh reaction above all from the Catholic cantons. Until the Catholics obtained a seat in the federal government (1891), religious peace was put to the test in Switzerland. During that period (called the "Kulturkampf"), arguments were often heated, such as in the Ticino Canton, where the Confederation had to directly intervene to mediate a furious conflict between Catholics and radical-liberals.

34-35 The International Red Cross was created to alleviate the suffering of the wounded in war after the Battle of Solferino. In Geneva, in the 1920s, Red-Cross workers were concerned with the hygiene of abandoned children.

35 bottom The flag of the International Red Cross is the opposite of the Swiss one: a red emblem on a white background. In the photo, nurses wait for the wounded in battle at the Geneva station, at the end of the First World War.

36 top In 1931, the first international banking institution, the Bank of International Settlements, designed to ameliorate the catastrophic economic and financial situation caused by the First World War, was founded in Basel.

36 center Swiss soldiers defended their nation's frontiers from potential invasion by Axis forces throughout the Second World War.

Even mountain borders were monitored.

36 bottom During spring of 1945, many prisoners of war or forced laborers sought to enter Switzerland and take refuge. In the photo, the roadway of St. Margrethen that connects Switzerland and Austria.

36-37 After the Great War (1914-1918), many civilian prisoners were repatriated.

Switzerland came unprepared to the outburst of the First World War. From an economic point of view, the country suffered greatly from being completely encircled by belligerent countries and from not having predicted the eventuality of a long war. Though the Swiss army proved itself to be efficient at guarding the borders, the situation with export industries was problematical. It got to the point where food products were being rationed and train schedules were even cancelled one day a week because coal was scarce. Economic disparity in the country grew and, at the end of the war, serious social tensions were added to regional ones that saw Romansch Switzerland and German Switzerland taking opposite sides (with Germany and with Italy respectively) in the conflict. Additionally, in 1918, because of extremists operating within the socialist party (Lenin himself, who was in Switzerland, contributed to the radicalization of the movement), the situation deteriorated and a general strike was declared; it was put down by the Swiss army. The period allowed the socialists, Catholics, and upper-class farmland owners (who had separated from the liberals) to achieve important victories. In 1919, a second Catholic conservative joined the federal government and, ten years later, the first representative of the agricultural party.

The Treaty of Versailles confirmed Swiss neutrality, which, in the period between the two wars, had wavered between openness and closure. Thanks to the active commitment of the federal councilor Giuseppe Motta, the people quickly approved joining the League of Nations, which had its headquarters in Geneva. Nonetheless, in 1938, with the Second World War imminent, not wanting to consent to obligatory participation in United Nations sanctions against Mussolini's Italy, Switzerland reinstated full neutrality.

Switzerland was also subject to the heavy repercussions of the world economic crisis of 1929. The watchmaking and tourism industries were severely hit. Exports experienced a collapse, while unemployment rose to significant levels. The franc had to be devaluated by 30 percent. The crisis forced the Confederation to give aid to industries and to adopt a series of social measures. Such policies, combined with a shift of the left in a social-democratic sense, stifled the class struggle and led the social parties to underwrite, in 1937, the so-called "labor peace." Union and employers organizations worked to resolve future conflicts through negotiations

and reconciliation. This spirit – well rooted in the Swiss tradition of arbitration – brought about the settlement of collective contracts in several economic sectors and laid the foundations for a model that, as of the post-Second-World-War period, would produce economic development and widespread prosperity.

The Second World War did not find Switzerland unprepared as it had been for the first. The militia army was well organized and the military budget ready to sustain a long conflict. The commander of the troops, General Henri Guisan, could count on the unanimous support of the various Swiss regions and was able to ensure a united front between the army and the population. The pro-Fascists and political-front supporters lost momentum, and in 1943, a socialist joined the federal government, thus consolidating the country's political equilibrium. Despite these conditions, when Switzerland found itself completely surrounded by the Axis powers and the occupied countries (France and Austria), the situation became quite difficult. The Swiss government agreed to not concede refugee status to Jews persecuted for racial reasons. By 1938, it had asked the German Reich to fix a seal of identification to the passports of Jews from Germany and, claiming "the boat to be full," refused numerous fugitives at the border, who thereafter encountered persecution. Though the population and union and Christian associations (especially south of the Alps, along the border with Italy) provided generous hospitality to a many victims of political persecution and to Jews, the attitude of the federal authorities (apart from some commendable exceptions) proved to be very restrictive. Swiss industries collaborated with the economy of the Reich, including those sectors funding the war, and banks opened their vaults to the German gold, even though it had been, in part, stolen from the occupied countries and victims of the Holocaust.

What can be said of the behavior of the Swiss political authorities? In-depth research on the period sponsored by Switzerland itself has established that, among other things, the Swiss government – fearing a truly dramatic situation and the persistent threat of invasion by the Axis powers – was essentially led during the war by the persons managing the economic and financial sectors. The government did not take care, immediately after the war, to ensure that question of the assets of Holocaust victims sitting in Swiss banks was settled quickly and appropriately.

OUI

À L'EEE, CAR LES FEMMES, REGARDENT L'AVENIR EN FACE.

FEMMES SUISSES EN FAVEUR DE L'EEE

The Swiss economy did not directly suffer the devastating consequences of the Second World War, and took off when the conflict ended. The gross national product soared and salaries doubled, riding the wave of development in the watchmaking, pharmaceutical, and confectionary/food-stuff industries. In the meantime, the foundations of a complex social-security system were drafted: pension, life-insurance, and worker's-compensation programs were instituted, and soon thereafter, insurance against illness and obligatory unemployment insurance. Demographic growth was fast: in the space of a generation, the population increased from 4.2 million inhabitants (1941) to 6.3 million (1971). As of the 1970s, a lack of manual labor started to emerge that attracted heavy immigration from Mediterranean countries (Italy, Spain, and then Portugal) to Switzerland. Once integrated, the immigrant population contributed to further increasing the demographic growth curve and to reinforcing the welfare system. Immigration brought about the launching of a series of initiatives meant to limit the foreign population, but they were not approved by popular vote.

From a political point of view, in 1959 a second representative from the socialist party joined the federal council. The federal government was thus composed of two radical liberals, two Christian Democrats, two socialists, and a representative from the agrarian party, later renamed the Central Democratic Union. Recent electoral success of the latter party with their layperson accents led them, in 2003, to win another seat in the government, to the detriment of the Democratic Christians that now had only one representative.

The policy of neutrality that Switzerland strictly observe during the 20th century did not mean that it remained at a distance from international organizations. Geneva became the United Nations' main European headquarters, as well as that of the numerous other international entities in the social and humanitarian fields, organizations that Switzerland has joined.

The role that the International Committee of the Red Cross played during the Second World War and in the second half of the last century has been of great importance. Swiss humanitarian aid and cooperation in the development of third-world countries has continued to increase further in recent decades, echoing the motto "neutrality and solidarity," which still drives Swiss foreign policy today. Despite that, the Swiss people, who voted to join the International Monetary Fund and the World Bank in 1992, approved the proposal to join the United Nations as a full member only in 2002, after years of reluctance. Moreover, they are in no hurry to join the European Union. A member for decades of the European Free Trade Association (EFTA), Switzerland has refused to enter the European Economic Zone, preferring to adopt bilateral accords with the European Union, which were approved in 2000 by a wide majority. These have made it possible for the Confederation to participate in the Union's free market without, however, having to give up its sovereignty and its own political institutions, beginning with its system of direct democracy.

40-41 The Alpine massif occupies a considerable part of Swiss territory. There are many landscapes of a totally pristine, rare beauty, the preferred destination of experienced mountaineers in both summer and winter.

Switerland's location in the middle of a continent and the dominance of the Alpine Massif heavily affect the nation's environment conditions. The Alps represent a demarcation line from a climatic and hydrological point of view. The majority of the Swiss territory is located north of the Alps and has a moderately humid climate. To the south, on the other hand, the climate and vegetation are more Mediterranean in nature. The Swiss Alps also function as the continent's watershed. The sources of the Rhine and Rhône rivers are found there, as well as those of some of the tributaries of the Po (e.g., the Ticino River) and the Danube (e.g., the Inn River). Of the total water volume, 68 percent drains off into the Rhine and ends up in the North Sea; 28 percent ends up in the Mediterranean Sea via the Rhône, Po, and Adige rivers, and the remaining 4 percent flows into the Black Sea by way of the Inn and Danube rivers.

During the ice ages, glaciers heavily modified the landscape, and many lakes were formed at the base of the Alps, both to the north and to the south, and the Jura. In recent times many more lakes have been added on the Alpine Massif itself, for use in the production of hydroelectric energy. Water is a fundamental resource, and Switzerland's hot springs (from the historic ones at Baden to the more recently developed ones at Leukerbad, Vals and elsewhere) are famous throughout the world. However, water, watercourses and springs also represents a great threat in terms of floods and landslides, above all in the alpine and sub-alpine areas.

Switzerland can be divided into five geographical zones: the Alps, the northern Prealps, the southern Prealps, the Swiss Plateau, and the Jura. It has a total surface area of only 15,398 square miles, and the Alps (some 200 miles in breadth) occupy a very extensive but largely unproductive swathe of territory. At high altitudes, there is no vegetation whatsoever. At medium altitudes, there are meadows and coniferous forests. Some of the big alpine valleys are very fertile, like those of the Rhône and the Rhine. The northern Prealps are a transitional zone with medium-high, sparsely populated mountains and vast green expanses (precipitation is relatively high) where raising livestock is the major farming activity. The Plateau, which is fairly narrow (from 30 to 60 miles in breadth) is a densely populated area that stretches from Lake Geneva (Lac Léman) to Lake Constance (the Bodensee). Switzerland's main urban centers, most fertile farming lands, and biggest industrial complexes are concentrated on the Plateau. It ends at the Jura range, which runs from west to northwest and which is shaped on one side by crests running north-south separated by narrow valleys and on the other by flat-topped mountainous formations. Coniferous forests abound. South of the Alps, in the Ticino Valley and around the lakes and in some valleys of the Grisons, the vegetation and the climate are almost Mediterranean. In this region, 37 percent of the surface area is productive agricultural land, 30 percent is forested, and remaining third is unproductive – rocks, lakes, and waterways). More than half the territory of the Valais and Uri Cantons and almost half of the Grisons Canton, which are alpine regions, do not produce anything at all.

41 top right The great expanse of this Andermatt area pastureland attests to a wild natural setting tamed by man because of the need to raise and bring livestock to pasture, a livelihood that still represents the main source of income for many Swiss mountain dwellers.

42 top left The view ranges across the imposing Aletsch Glacier, which with its 54 square miles of surface area is the biggest in all the Alps and the longest in Europe.

42 top right Above 6500 ft (2000 m), the Alps are covered by giant glaciers that, over millions of years, with their quiet strength, have transformed a large part of Switzerland's landscape.

42-43 For a good part of the year, vast valley floors, impervious rock walls and snowy peaks largely characterize the Bernese Oberland. The configuration of the terrain shows the unmistakable traces left behind by the glaciers' withdrawal.

43 bottom Plaine Morte Glacier, straddling the Bernese and Valais Alps, is a 4-sq.-mile white field surrounded by rocks and crags; it inspires great awe and calls for absolute silence.

44-45 Among the most imposing glaciers, the Gornergletscher extends all around the Monte Rosa massif. It stands out for its vastness and length, reaching up to seven miles.

The Alps, the Plateau, and the Jura each have rocks with very different characteristics. The St. Gotthard Massif and the Bernese Alps are composed predominantly of granite and crystalline rock. The Val Bregaglia, south of the Grisons, is made up of a younger granite. In the Ticino Valley, gneiss is predominant on the massif. These rocks produce pure crystals of extraordinary beauty. In the northern Alps (Mt. Pilatus and the Säntis), there are calcareous sediments with layers of sandstone. In the Glarus Alps and the eastern Plateau, red and green mineral sediments are found. The characteristic rock of the Plateau is however *molasses* (fossiliferous sedimentary deposits), soft and deeply gouged by rivers. In northwestern and southernmost Switzerland (in the Jura and southern Ticino) on the other hand, calcareous rock is abundant. Some of these sedimentation patterns (particularly in the Rhine region of Basel and Rheinfelden) contain important reserves of rock salt, widely exploited for the national production of salt.

As mentioned earlier, the Swiss countryside has been shaped by the movement of the glaciers. Of the ancient ones of the Rhône, Rhine, Ticino, Linth, Reuss, and Aare, which once covered a large part of the territory, remarkable patches still remain today: more than 200 square miles, dominated by the Aletsch Glacier, Europe's largest at 15 miles long, with a surface area of 33 square miles (54, if the Oberaletsch's – which is 5.5 miles long – is included). Also noteworthy are the Bernese glacier of the Unteraare (8.6 miles long) and the Morteratsch of the Grisons (5.2 miles). In general, the rocks that were covered by glaciers have rounder and smoother shapes. The indented peaks mark the highest altitudes reached by the glaciers. At the points were they used to come together, covering the peaks, they formed hollows and passes. In the alpine regions, the erosive action of the principal and secondary glaciers has created somewhat large, primary valleys and terraced or cascading secondary valleys. Where the rock was harder, deep gorges formed (those of Schöllenen and Viamala are famous). Where it was softer, the glaciers created vast valley floors, especially suited to human settlement, or lakes. The residual debris produced lateral or frontal moraines or rolling hills of gravel. Then, thanks to the action of the waterways produced by the thaw, the valleys of the Plateau became home to huge sand, clay, and gravel deposits. Indisputable evidence of the passage of the glaciers are the great randomly located rocks, one of which stands symbolically at the northern exit of the St. Gotthard Highway.

46 top left Lake Constance forms the border between Switzerland and Germany. It is only a political border: the roofs, houses, and domes of the churches reflect a single style and culture.

46 top right Spiez Castle – a few miles from Bern – with its giant tower seems to compete with the peaks of the mountains of the Bernese Oberland, which acts as a splendid natural crown to Thun Lake.

The continental watershed separates the rivers that flow into the southern seas from those that end in the North Sea and the Atlantic. This line passes through Switzerland in a highly original way. On one side, there is the Rhine Valley, which carries the run-off of the majority of Swiss-born waters and forms an arc from the central Alps as far as Lake Constance, making a sharp turn at Basel to then aim resolutely for the North Sea. On the other side, the head-streams of the Rhône and the tributaries of the Po, Adige, and Danube send their waters toward the Mediterranean and Black seas. At the crest of the Bernina Pass, in the Grisons, the watershed is easily visible; the White and Black lakes mark the demarcation line in an almost iconic way (a sight Proust noted with joy when he visited the area). The three longest rivers rising in Swiss territory are the Rhine (233 miles), the Aare (183 miles), and the Rhône (164 miles). The upper Rhine collects the waters from eastern Switzerland. The

Aare, on the other hand, is the collection basin for the most important rivers of the plateau and then also for the Reuss and Limmat rivers, before in turn flowing into the Rhine itself. Other waterways hold a certain importance: the Linth-Limmat (87 miles), the Sarine (which acts as a linguistic border as well, 79 miles), the Inn (64 miles), the Ticino (56 miles), the Broye (53 miles), the Doubs (in the Jura), 46 miles, the Sihl (near Zürich) 45 miles, and the Maggia (35 miles). Switzerland has numerous lakes. On the Plateau between the two big basins of Lake Geneva (Lac Léman, 224 sq. miles) and Lake Constance (the Bodensee, 209 sq. miles), are the lakes of Zürich (35 sq. miles) and Zug (15 sq. miles), Neuchâtel (84 sq. miles), Bienne (15 sq. miles), and Morat (9 sq. miles). In the Prealps are the lakes of Thun (19 sq. miles), Brienz (12 sq. miles), and of the Four Cantons (Lake Lucerne, 44 sq. miles). South of the Alps are Lake Locarno (Lake Maggiore, 82 sq. miles) and Lake Lugano (19 sq. miles).

46 bottom The placid shores of Lake Geneva in the Veveyse region are covered by wide terraces planted with vineyards, land that for centuries has produced white wines appreciated in Switzerland and abroad.

47 An avenue of cypress trees rings the calm waters of Lake Lugano; a neoclassical villa is immersed in the luxuriant natural setting south of the Alps. Switzerland is made up of contrasts: the Mediterranean softness of the lakes opposes the hardness of the mountains.

48 top The River Aare descends from the Bernese Alps and grows rapidly thanks to the numerous mountain streams that swell its waters, going on to broaden before flowing through Bern.

48 bottom At the level of Lake Constance the Rhine is channeled into dykes before its waters blend into those of the largest lake on Swiss territory.

48-49 The Rhine runs north from the Alps, crossing all of eastern and part of northern Switzerland. In the photo, one of the many bridges that span it along its course.

50-51 In the Andermatt region, an area nestled onto the St. Gotthard massif, meadows abound, dotted by alpine dairies that make a cheese with an unmistakable alpine-grass flavor.

50 top In some famous places like the Kleine Scheidegg, at the base of the Jungfrau, summer visitors are almost as numerous as winter ones. The unmistakable alpine vegetation delights the hikers.

51 top Cows at pasture are one of the symbols of Switzerland. With their bells, they evoke the idea of an idyllic life, far from the noise and chaos that grip urban areas.

Interesting karstic phenomena appear in the alpine regions of Schwyz and Glarus, and also frequently in the Jura. Karst, a calcareous rock, is very permeable. This permeability has led to the formation of crevasses and underground reservoirs, such as that feeding the springs of Orbe). It is not rare in the karst regions to find underground caves, often with gorgeous stalactites. In the Muotathal Valley, the network of underground caves of the so-called Hölloch (Hell Hole) is probably Europe's most extensive.

Different climatic conditions exist in the various Swiss geographical zones: in the west, maritime; in the east, continental; in the north, sub-polar; and in the south, Mediterranean. Climatic diversity also affects the landscapes, highly varied for such a small country. The vegetation changes even on the basis of altimetric jumps. At lower levels (up to the limits of vineyards, about 2000 feet), there is a mittel-European and Mediterranean climate in the southern areas of Italian Switzerland but even steppe-like grass in the Valais. In the valleys where the *föhn* blows, plants that prefer hot temperatures and alpine plants grow side by side. Up to 3900 feet, leafy forests (beech and some firs or Scotch pines) prevail. From 3900 to 5900 feet is the realm of the conifers: larches, silver firs, spruce trees, and Swiss stone pines. From 5900 to 6500 feet is the truly alpine band, the one with the real meadows, where in summer cows and goats are brought to pasture and edelweiss, bluebells, and blueberries grow. Above this altitude, alpine vegetation similar to that of the tundra grows up to 8200 feet; higher up, there is only rock and snow.

52 top Piz Medel, in the Grisons Alps, seems unattainable. Yet, its peak is accessible even in winter, both by expert climbers as well as fit hikers and lovers of high-altitude skiing.

Any guide in Curaglia will accompany an enthusiast up to the Medel Hut (at 8200 ft/2500 m) and then on to the top. Skiing down it is unforgettable.

52-53 In the area of the well-known resort town of Verbier, in the Valais Canton, the veil of the clouds is pierced to reveal a magnificent setting in a practically pristine mountain environment.

Switzerland's great alpine peaks are an attraction known worldwide. The majority of the peaks that rise above 13,000 feet are found in the Valais Canton: the Matterhorn (14,688 feet), Monte Rosa (15,200 feet), the Weisshorn (14,776 feet), the Dent Blanche (14,291 feet), the Grand Combin (14,150 feet), and the Aletschhorn (13,760 feet). In the Bern Canton, what may be the most visited massif is located: the Jungfrau , (13,638 feet), flanked by the Eiger and the Mönch. In the Grisons, there is Piz Bernina (13,281 feet). The Swiss mountains are also an extraordinary crossroads between northern and southern Europe via its passes: Great St. Bernard (connecting the Valais with Italy), St. Gotthard ("the Way of the Peoples"), the Nufenen, Furka, Grimsel, and Susten passes (linking Italian Switzerland and Uri with the Valais and Bern), San Bernardino, Lukmanier, Splügen, Julier, and Albula, roads connecting the Grisons with Italy, and, internally, between the Rhine Valley and the Engadin.

53 At 13,331 ft (4060 m), the Obergabelhorn is one of the highest peaks in the Valais Alps. Located in the Zermatt region, it is a companion worthy of the Matterhorn, Monte Rosa, the Grand Combin, and other peaks of over 13,000 ft about this unique region.

54 top The Furka Pass connects the Reuss Valley (which starts in the St. Gotthard massif) and that of the Rhône. This pass, one of the most enchanting in all of the Alps, offers great views of the imposing and massive Rhône glacier.

54 bottom The Julier Pass was known to the Romans, who used it as a military and commercial route from north to south. Several traces from the Roman era have been found in the area of the pass, which links the Rhine valley to that of the River Inn (from which comes the name Engadin).

54-55 Piz Bernina, the Cambrena, and the glacier of the same name stand out above the White Lake, near the rest area where the Bernina Hostel (7392 ft/2250 m) stands, in the upper Engadin. At this transition point between the Valtellina and Switzerland, the Romans once stopped to refresh themselves, spend the night, and change their horses.

55 top left Since Roman times, the Simplon Pass has been an important route between the Po River valley and the upper Rhône. The first statutes governing the transport of goods were drafted in 1321. Between 1801 and 1805, Napoleon had a new road with 611 bridges and 1723 ft (525 m) of tunnels built over the route of the old mule track.

55 top right The Great St. Bernard Hostel (8111 ft/2470 m), a safe shelter for those traveling over the pass, was built in 1045 by Bernard of Mentone, a monk and saint, whose statue overlooks the building. The first dogs were brought by monks in the 17th century: their special abilities made them able to find and save travelers lost or buried in the snow.

56-57 Monte Rosa, whose unmistakable profile and magic colors are so familiar to the inhabitants of Lombardy, the Val d'Aosta, and Piedmont, is one of the most majestic peaks in the Alps. Dufour Point (15,204 ft/4634 m) falls short of Mont Blanc by only 500 ft (150 m(or so. Its main crest is the border between Switzerland and Italy.

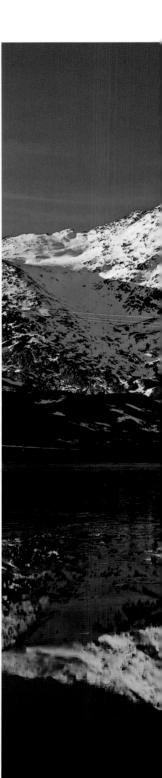

58 top left The well-known mountain resort of St. Moritz is not just the preferred destination of lovers of skiing: groups of climbers armed with ice axes, crampons, and ropes scaling the faces of the Engadin, situated like a crown around the little town, are numerous.

58 top right Climbing from Pontresina, near St. Moritz, towards the Bernina Pass, one's gaze is attracted by the Morterasch Glacier, a destination for many climbers wishing to train in an environment that does not feature any too severe challenges.

The Engadin – where the Inn River runs, from the Maloja Pass to Scuoland to the border – has a much different configuration than that of the other alpine valleys, generally more deeply entrenched. It is at a high altitude (it varies from 4900 to 5900 feet) but the valley floor is wide open, sprinkled with little lakes, like those of Silvapalana, Sils, and St. Moritz. Known throughout the world as a winter and summer resort, St. Moritz (5900 feet) is surrounded by peaks like Piz Corvatsch (11,320 feet) and Piz Murtel (11,260 feet) and is the intersection for routes leading to the Bernina Massif, to the Diavolezza, and to the Morteratsch Glacier. The lakes are popular in summer with hikers and in winter with cross-country skiers and tourists on horseback. From Zernez, in the Lower Engadin, the visitor can enter the Swiss National Park, which covers a territory of 66 sq. miles, with altitudes ranging from 4600 feet to 10,500 feet above sea level, between the Inn River valley, the Val Müstair, and the Fuorn Pass. In the nature reserve, animals (deer, roe deer, ibex, marmots, bearded vultures, and more) and plants (bluebells, edelweiss, and rare alpine species) are strictly protected, and the hand of man does not intervene even to clear out dead trees. From the 50 miles of paths with instructional signs in five languages, hikers can admire the majestic countryside and enjoy a unique show of vegetation.

58-59 Of all Swiss fortresses, Tarasp Castle, built upon a rock spur, near Scuol in the lower Engadin Valley, is among the most imposing and famous. The lords of Tarasp, who came to the Engadin from the region of Lake Como, settled there in the 11th century.

59 top Charming valleys at the base of the Corvatsch (a famous ski resort) and Roseg peaks ascend from lakes Champfer and Silvaplana: enchanting sites for summer and winter day trips, they can be reached by horse-drawn sleighs.

60-61 An ancient city with hot springs, by the mid-1800s, St. Moritz had become a resort for elite European visitors (above all during the winter). Located in the heart of the upper Engadin, it is the departure point for famous alpine destinations such as Diavolezza, the Corvatsch, and the Bernina.

63 top left Roe deer are numerous on the peaks. In the mountains, it is not uncommon to see them nimbly jumping from rock to rock with an extraordinary sense of balance, or standing on a peak, undaunted by the sheer drop below.

63 top right Rocks above 6500 ft (2000 m) are inhabited by alpine species, particularly the ibex, which has been adopted as the emblem of the Grisons Canton. It is not a protected species: the so-called "high hunt" actually acts to regulate the population of these hoofed creatures on the territory.

62 top Entire colonies of marmots live in extensive underground dens under high-altitude meadows. They come out with their little ones but call them back with their typical high-pitched whistle as soon as they hear or smell a threatening presence or an approaching human.

62 bottom A face-off between capercailzie, or Old World grouse. Switzerland has an estimated thousand of this extremely rare birds that prefer rarefied coniferous forests, where light easily filters through the foliage.

62-63 Characteristic of alpine regions below 6500 ft (2000 m) are large coniferous forests and small alpine lakes fed by melting snow in the summer: some artificial ones have been created to produce hydro-electric power.

The Rhine is without a doubt the waterway that, for its power and length, has the most impact of any on Swiss territory. After leaving large Lake Constance, near Schaffhausen, the river – over 390 feet wide at this point – plunges over a 70-foot waterfall. The Rhine Falls are the most impressive in Europe and have fired the imaginations of visitors and poets throughout the centuries. The Plateau is differentiated by its lush pastures and rolling hills. In the Einsiedeln area, there are vast expanses of peat bogs like that at Rothenthurm, the green hills of Appenzell and Toggenburg, soft valleys like the Emmenthal (not far from Bern), and picturesque lakes (in the region around Bienne, Morat, and Neuchâtel). Near the eastern and central Prealps, the hills give way to peaks like the Säntis (8200 feet) or the imposing Mt. Pilatus (6983 feet). In the Fribourg Prealps, the massive spur of the Moléson (6569 feet) is the counterpoint to the lush pastures of the Gruyère (known throughout the world, since they produce the cheese of the same name).

The Jura range forms a natural barrier between the Swiss Plateau, France, and Germany. It is a long and variable panoramic balcony of pastureland, forest, and rocks, interrupted by deep, twisting valleys, through which the Doubs, Suze, and Birz rivers run. In some areas, the climate can be rather severe (the Brévine, in the Val de Travers, is called the Swiss Siberia). At the farthest end of northern Jura, the peak of the Chasseral (5273 feet) offers an extraordinary panoramic view of the Alps.

64 top The spur of Mt. Pilatus Kulm (6995 ft/2132 m), near Lucerne, is one of the most popular destinations for visitors. Once at the top, thanks to a cable car and a small rack-and-pinion railway, they can enjoy a truly unique panoramic view of the Lake of the Four Cantons and the Alps.

64 bottom The faces of the Pilatus are unyielding, with breathtaking sheer cliffs. Nonetheless, the inhabitants of the Catholic canton of Lucerne had the chapel of Klimsenhorn built there, where on August 15 they celebrate the feast of the Virgin Mary.

64-65 Growing ever more swollen, the Rhine flows from the Grisons Alps to Lake Constance as far as Basel. It then crosses Germany and gushes into the North Sea. At Schaffhausen, it has already acquired remarkable force, and its waterfalls, which can be approached by boat, are impressive.

65 top Switzerland is not only mountains and a plateau. It is also a land of lakes, as can clearly be seen in the waterways that originate in the alpine region. The biggest is Lake Constance (the Bodensee), which forms the border between Switzerland and Germany.

The so-called Swiss Lemanic Riviera, stretching from Geneva to Lausanne to Montreux, is a residential shoreline lined by vineyards that descend toward the shore of Switzerland's biggest lake, an arc 45 miles long and up to 8 miles wide. The Rhône, still an impetuous alpine river, flows out of the Valais into the lake, and then flows out at Geneva to head tranquilly toward France. From Mt. Pélérin and the hills that form a crown around the lake, the visitor gaze can range as far as Geneva, the lower Valais, and France.

The Rhône's upper valley, from Lake Geneva to the Furka Pass, is a microcosm unto itself. Linked to the rest of the country by Lake Geneva, the Nufenen and Furka passes, and to Italy through Simplon and the Great St. Bernard Pass, the Valais has been furrowed by the great river and scored by heavy glaciers and their debris. Its peaks include some of the most beautiful in the Alps, beginning with the instantly recognizable Matterhorn and the threatening Diablerets. Its winter and summer resorts (Villars, Montana, and Zermatt) are famous. Its lateral valleys (Hérens, Anniviers) have maintained their old charm, with villages at high altitudes (Chandolin, one of the highest in Europe, is at 6353 feet) that feature the typical *châlet*, *raccard*, and *mazot* (elevated granaries) with stone roofs.

The Valaisian Alps border on the equally majestic ones of the Bern Canton, entered by way of Interlaken, via Grindelwald. The Jungfrau massif – including the Eiger, Mönch, and the Aletsch Glacier (straddling the Valais) – numbers among the Heritage of Humanity sites listed by UNESCO.

68-69 The Rhône valley, spacious and sunny, slowly descends until meeting into Lake Geneva. Plantations of orchards and vineyards, which continue down along the shores of the lake almost as far as Geneva, are characteristic.

69 top Martigny (the ancient Octodurus), the capital of southern Valais and the bishop's seat during the early Christian era, was for centuries custodian of the road leading to St. Bernard. Today, it is a hard-working city, known for its excellent art exhibitions.

69 bottom The abundant vineyards of the Valais and the lake shores of the Veveyse as far as Lausanne produce noteworthy wines: Saint-Saphorin or the rare and prized Petite Arvine attest to the generous sunshine that these areas enjoy.

70 top left Beyond the Rhône Valley and the Simplon Pass, a series of lateral valleys commences, overlooked by the tallest peaks in the Valais and in Switzerland, including Monte Rosa and the Matterhorn. The first of the valleys are Saas Fee and Saas Grund, a paradise for winter skiers.

70 top right The Eiger (13,026 ft/3982 m), overlooking Grindelwald in the Bernese Alps, along with the Mönch and the Jungfrau compose the legendary trio now inscribed on UNESCO'S Heritage of Humanity List. The Eiger's north face is still a highly popular destination for all climbers.

70-71 Zermatt can be reached by way of a valley or through Raron from the south. Once past St. Niklaus and Randa, the visitor approaches Täsch. From here, a rack-and-pinion railway goes to the village at the base of the Matterhorn. In addition to the stupendous view it affords of this gem of the Alps, Täsch is one big pedestrian zone.

71 top Spectacular peaks including the Wetterhorn, the Eiger, the Mönch, and the Jungfrau form an unforgettable setting for the village of Grindelwald, one of Switzerland's first resort towns, popular since the 17th century.

71 bottom The Jungfraujoch's peak offers an astounding panorama. A rack-and-pinion railway takes visitors up to 11,333 ft (3454 m) via tunnels pierced through rock. The station, the continent's highest, is called "Top of Europe."

72 top The valley that descends from Andermatt to Göschenen in the Reuss valley, grows narrow. Since Roman times numerous bridges have been built there, some are legendary – "the Devil's Bridge." Today road and railway tunnels serve travelers.

72 center The landscape south of the Alps is much different from that of central Switzerland. With its heavily populated slopes, Mt. Bré looks onto Lake Lugano, with its already Mediterranean climate and vegetation.

The region of the so-called "Lake of Four Cantons," or Lake Lucerne, is the geographical and historical heart of Switzerland. Around its shores, Uri, Schwyz, and Unterwalden formed the earliest nucleus of the Confederation. The outline of the lake, set between the tall peaks of the Titlis and Pilatus and the spurs of the Mythen, is really odd. All around are numerous grassy balconies (the very meadow where the legendary vow of the Rütli Confederation took place looks directly onto the lake). Here, the so-called "Way of the Peoples," the road begins that descends from the St. Gotthard Pass south of the Alps, which has made a lasting impression on many travelers. Beyond the gorges of the Schöllenen carved out by the Reuss River and the old "Devil's Bridge," near Andermatt, and past the St. Gotthard Pass, the landscape opens to the south onto the Ticino Valley.

Italian Switzerland is a region of picturesque prealpine valleys, lakes, and terraces covered by vineyards. Lake Locarno (Lake Maggiore) enjoys a mild climate where hydrangeas, magnolia trees, and camellias grow in spring. The islands of Brissago compose a vast botanical garden. Lake Lugano, whose waters border on Italy, is surrounded by the Bré, San Salvatore, Generoso, and San Giorgio mountains, the last mountains of the southern Swiss Prealps before the plains of the Po River valley.

72 bottom Sprawled over a large plain that begins at the base of the St. Gotthard Massif and ends below the Furka Pass, the village of Andermatt has long been an obligatory point of passage for travelers, merchants, and armies.

72-73 From Mt. Pilatus, the view encompasses the "Lake of the Four Cantons" (Lake Lucerne). The four cantons are the original ones of Uri, Schwyz, Obwald, and Unterwalden.

73 top From Andermatt, a train departs that, via the Oberalp Pass, connects the Uri Canton with the Grisons Canton and the Reuss valley with the Rhine valley. It is a high-altitude train that, with its various stops, makes it possible for visitors to travel right through the Alps, from the Valais to the Engadin.

CITIES: SMALL IS BEAUTIFUL

75 top right
Built in the area of
Bern, capital of the
Confederation, Thun
is a cheerful lake
town. The Brienz and
Thun lakes collect the
waters that rush
down from the Alps.

74 bottom A city of Roman origin, known for its hot springs, Baden has preserved many traces of its past. The castle, church, and town hall all attest to its role in Swiss history. The city enjoys an important position in industry, thanks to the Brown and Boveri families.

74-75 The extraordinary painted façades of the houses in Stein am Rhein reveal a rich and glorious past. The convent of St. George and the Hohenklingen castle looming over the town recall its medieval history, largely shaped by the dukes of Zähringen and the Bishopric of Bamberg.

75 top left The fortunes of Zug depend on its proximity to Zürich. The city entered the Confederation because it was strategically located on the road linking Zürich to Lucerne and the St. Gotthard Pass. Its modern-day development is directly tied to that of the financial markets centered in Zürich.

Switzerland has six urban centers. Four are located along its east-west axis: Zürich (with one million inhabitants within its metropolitan area), Bern (350,000), Lausanne (320,000), and Geneva (480,000). The other two, Basel (500,000) and Lugano (120,000, including all its suburbs), basically act as the northern and southern gateways to the country. Outside these important urban areas, the other cities are numerous but small in size. They developed during the Middle Ages around monasteries, the ruins of a few fortified Roman citadels, and the castles and palaces of noble families. The origins of the first urban settlements are all linked to political and commercial motives. The Zähringen, Kyburg, and Hapsburg, and Savoyard dynasties all wanted to strengthen their power in the region of the alpine arc and so each set up cities through-

out the territory. The Zähringens founded Fribourg on the Sarine River and Bern on the Aare River, and the towns of Morat, Thun, and Burgdorf. The counts of Kyburg founded Aarau, Lenzburg, Zug, and Frauenfeld. The Hapsburgs built Baden, Bremgarten, and Brugg, and the Savoy dynasty the cities of Romont and Yverdon in the highlands and Aigle and Morges between the Rhône and the banks of Lake Geneva. For conspicuously economic reasons, important cities like Geneva, Constance (and, in that area, Stein am Rhein), Lucerne, Zug, Thun, and Zürich grew at the junction of rivers and lakes.

In addition to the monks of St. Gallen – who were responsible for the city of the same name, which radiated out around the abbey – the bishops of Basel also founded the cities of Bienne and, in the Jura, Porrentruy and St. Ursanne.

76 top Montebello castle, whose walls are surrounded by vineyards, overlooks the city of Bellinzona. It turrets perfectly coordinate with those of Castelgrande, a second fortress. Much higher up and smaller in size towers the castle of Sasso Corbaro.

76-77 The castles of Bellinzona, part of UNESCO's Heritage of Humanity List, were built at the entrance to two passes of great strategic importance during the Middle Ages, the Lukmanier and St. Gotthard.

The structure of the medieval cities has been maintained roughly intact, as is seen in Morat, with its clear division of spaces among the church, castle, main streets, and walls, or Burgdorf and Thun, which stand at the base of the rise topped by the monumental castle.

Between the 15th and 16th centuries, a vast expansion of the city walls and fortifications took place. In Lucerne, the imposing tower of the Musegg was built, overlooking the city. In Bellinzona, on the site of ancient Roman fortifications, the Sforza and Visconti families built three castles to watch over an enormously strategic passage south of the Alps (all three have been entered by UNESCO on the Heritage of Humanity List). Important fortifications were also erected on the shores of lakes and rivers (the Wasserturm in Lucerne, the towers on the Sarine, in Fribourg, and the imposing fortified complex of Chillon Castle, a Savoyard manor dating back to the 12th century, are all famous). With the evolution of warfare, the towers of Swiss cities also changed in the 16th century: the rounded Basler Tor in Solothurn, the socalled Munot of Schaffhausen (a cylinder over 160 feet wide), or fortresses like the Elisabethenschanze in Basel, which hid sets of heavy artillery, are all remarkable.

In many Swiss cities, the city walls and various fortifications were razed to the ground in the 19th century, as they were considered a legacy of the Dark Ages and aristocratic society. In their place, green areas and public buildings were built.

In Zürich, a cantonal school, university, and the Polytechnic Institute were built and a walkway (the Hohe Promenade), tree-lined squares, and botanical gardens were created, in addition to big avenues and ring roads to deal with the new problem of traffic. In Basel, fortifications were replaced with wide avenues and the newly restored banks of the Rhine. In Geneva, the ancient defenses at the port gave way to public parks skirting the lake. Switzerland is a country of many rivers, and cities and towns often straddle watercourses. Bridges abound, from those built of wood from the Middle Ages (such as the Kapellbrücke in Lucerne) to the suspended cable bridges in Fribourg, later replaced by large viaducts.

78-79 Built by the dukes of Zähringen and based on a typical plan also found in Fribourg, the old city of Bern snuggles into a bend of the Aare River, and is connected to other city neighborhoods by big bridges.

78 top The streets of Fribourg's Old City descend parallel to each other from the street of the hospital and from the clock-tower toward the river flanking the cathedral. The façades of the medieval city end at the cobblestoned street with big arches and the typical below-street-level cellars.

79 left All of the
Old City is marked
by large towers
separating the streets
of the center. Bern, the
capital of Switzerland,
represents a living,
open-air museum,
which can be explored
on foot and by stopping
from time to time
before the main
buildings of its
political and
religious life.

BERN
CAPITAL OF
TWENTY-SIX CANTONS

The city was founded on the banks of the River Aare in 1191 by Duke Berthold V of Zähringen, riding the momentum created by the construction of Fribourg and Morat a few decades earlier. The coat-of-arms and the city's name originated with the fact that the first animal to be caught by the duke in these lands was a bear *(Bär)*. Having entered into the Swiss League in 1353, the city led an expansionist policy with great success. It conquered Aargau and part of the Vaud Canton, taking over the leadership and thus the heart of the Confederation.

The medieval city developed around the Gothic 15th- to 16th-century Gothic church of St. Vincent. This city, with its long parallel streets and multicolored fountains with allegorical statues at their center, extended out from the Zytglogge ("Clock-tower"). This is one of the oldest in Switzerland, and has a carillon that chimes the hours, which are marked by decorative moving figures.

79 right Bern's Town Hall is a masterpiece of the Gothic style, with its characteristic ogival vaults and pinnacled towers. In Switzerland, *the communes enjoy ample powers, and the capital's Town Hall has historically played a rather significant political role.*

80-81 The charm of the capital, with its bell-towers and the dome of the Federal Assembly Building all lit up, strikes many visitors. *During winter, a magical touch is added by the snow, which for several months accompanies the inhabitants of many Swiss cities.*

82-83 Among Bern's many monuments, the Zytglogge, the clock-tower dating back to the 12th century, is certainly the most admired with its big astronomical face and its moving puppets that rotate on the hour.

82 top left In bygone times, the Clock-Tower was one of the city's gateways. Today, visitors gather in small groups to watch the theatrical carousel with its automatic figurines.

82 top right St. Vincent's Cathedral, designed by Matthäus Ensinger (1421-1475) is in late-Gothic style.

Inside, there are priceless 15th-century stained-glass windows. The exterior flaunts a robust Flamboyant-style bell-tower.

83 top The façade of the Münster has three portals, and the Day of Judgment, with 234 partially-gilded characters on a colorful background, is painted on the gable.

83 right In the middle of the stone-paved streets of the historic center is a series of stone fountains topped by colorful allegorical figures, characters evoking a world in which images wielded a strong symbolic and educational effect.

Opposite the Zytglogge, at the western end of the Marktplatz, is the Käfigturm (Cage Tower), built in the 13th century. Both the historic towers have served as city gaols.

In the 19th century, Napoleon significantly cut Bern's territorial power down to size, but after his defeat at Waterloo in 1815, the Congress of Vienna compensated the Bern Canton, giving it the ancient principality of the bishop of Basel in the Jura. In 1848, at the time of the birth of the modern Helvetic Confederation, Bern was chosen to be the political capital of the new federal state.

The Bundeshaus (Federal Assembly Building) was begun in 1852 and built in two phases to the designs of Friedrich Studer and Hans Wilhelm Auer.

A city with military roots, surrounded by fertile countryside, Bern also has a rich intellectual and cultural history. It has been the birthplace or the academic home of many famous artists and scientists. Einstein worked on his theory of relativity while living in Bern and Paul Klee lived in Bern in his youth. The city has honored him with a striking museum designed by Renzo Piano, which contains the world's largest collection of Klee's work. Bern is also the hometown of the great Swiss painter Ferdinand Hodler (1853-1918), and the Bern Museum of Fine Arts devotes much space to the work of this master of symbolism and allegory.

84-85 The Federal Building, completed in 1902, was built according to a design by Hans Wilhelm Auer. The headquarters of the Swiss Parliament and government, the massive structure overlooks the River Aare to the north and faces onto Federal Square to the south.

85 top left Characteristic of the city of Bern, and in particular its historic center, are the numerous open-air restaurants conducive to socializing. Bern is a city where cordiality and hospitality reign supreme.

85 top right A bus named Einstein runs down the Spitalgasse, which connects the train station to the historic center; it celebrates the scientific genius Albert Einstein, an illustrious adoptive citizen of Bern.

84 top Bern boasts an ancient musical and artistic tradition. The marquee of the Stadttheater attracts lovers of music from the canton and from all over Switzerland.

84 center The hall of the National Council (Chamber of the People) is decorated with a fresco by Charles Giron (The Cradle of the Confederation) that illustrates the Rütli Meadow where the representatives of the early cantons swore loyalty in 1291. In the background are the peaks of the two Mythen.

84 bottom A walk through the streets of Bern reveals eleven historic fountains dating back to the mid-16th century. Among them is the Ogre Fountain in Kornhausplatz.

86-87 The Rhine is the uncontested lord of Basel. On its banks, a city of profitable ful commerce, not to mention great culture has developed over the centuries. This fertile ground shaped the inhabitants' character; they are cheerfully open to meeting new people from beyond their borders.

86 top The Old City still bears traces of its past. A Roman province, episcopal seat, and a renowned center for humanistic and scientific studies: all of these incarnations can be read on the walls of Basel's historic homes.

87 bottom left The Spalentor, a monumental fortified gate with two towers that give way to the moat around the base of the city walls, was built in the 14th century. From there, the university, the oldest in Switzerland, founded in 1460, can be reached down Spalengraben Street.

*87 bottom right
The artisans' quarter
evokes the feeling of
ancient medieval
workshops. This part
of the city dates back
to the 13th century,
which, in the Baroque
era, was brought
within the
fortifications built
at that time.*

BASEL
CROSSROADS
OF TRADE AND IDEAS

Basel, which is located in northern-most Switzerland on the banks of the Rhine and borders Alsace and the German state of Baden-Württemberg, is an industrial hub of great importance. The entire area of the present-day city was occupied by Roman garrisons until the 2nd century B.C. The cathedral has ancient origins (9th century), but the existing building was consecrated in the second half of the 14th century. After the construction of a bridge over the Rhine, at the beginning of the 13th century, Basel became a center for commerce between the north and south of the continent. The famous town hall, with its red façade, dominates the Marktplatz. In 1392, Basel was able to expand, acquiring so-called Little Basel, on the other side of the Rhine. This act marked the city's emancipation from the Hapsburgs. The city's border with its ancient suburb of Spalen is marked by the perfectly preserved Spalentor, built in the 14th century and known for its turrets and period sculptures.

The city became a European leader in paper and book making and one of the biggest centers for theological studies and humanistic learning. From 1431 to 1448, it hosted the Roman Catholic Church's Ecumenical Council; in 1460, when the city's university opened, it attracted scholars of the caliber of Erasmus of Rotterdam. The city has long been famed for its contri-

butions to science and mathematics; it was home to Bernoulli dynasty in the 17th century and to Leonard Euler, the greatest mathematical genius of 18th century.

Basel realized its commercial potential with the arrival of the Huguenots in the 17th and 18th centuries. It first became one of the capitals of the silk-weaving industry, ribbon manufacturing, and cloth dyeing. The earliest chemical industries sprang up at the end of the 18th century, with Geigy going into business in 1785, opening the path toward real specialization in this industry. In the 20th century, Basel became the headquarters of such pharmaceutical and chemical giants as Ciba, LaRoche, and later, Novartis. In addition to being a business center, Basel is an art-loving and cultural city. Its numerous museums, renowned for their prestigious collections, include the fine arts museum, the museum of contemporary art, and the museum of the whimsical 20th-century sculptor Jean Tinguely, not to mention to the Beyeler Foundation.

90 top right Basel's Town Hall was enlarged in the 17th century and the façade was altered. In 1900, the building's left wing and the tower on the right (as seen from the square) were added. The rear part dating back to the 14th century, was renovated.

90-91 The handsome rectangular block of the Town Hall, painted in shades of red, looks onto the Marktplatz (Market Square). Built in the 14th century, it is today the seat of the government of the Canton of Basel City. The local aristocracy wanted it built on this site as a distinctive gesture when viewed from Prince-Bishop's residence on the hill above the city.

91 top left Inside the Münster, the remains of the previous Romanesque construction can still be seen. The cloister contains numerous tombs of the city's most important families, and the remains of Erasmus of Rotterdam also rest there.

90 top left The roof of the Town Hall's tower is a little masterpiece recalling decorations like those on the Hospice de Beaune, in Burgundy. The tiles are multicolored.

90 center left Featured on the Town Hall's façade are the coats-of-arms of the twelve Swiss cantons composing the Helvetic Confederation of 1501. This is the year in which Basel joined the League of the Confederates, an act the city's artisan guilds strongly opposed.

90 bottom left The façade that we see today features trompe-l'oeil *architectural elements designed by Hans Bock. At the sides of the clock are frescoes of two guards holding, on the sides of their halberds, a shield with the canton's coat-of-arms.*

91 top right As early as the 9th century a place of worship stood on the hill looking onto Basel and the Rhine. In the 10th century, the Hungarians destroyed the Carolingian basilica; the present-day Gothic cathedral dates back to the second half of the 14th century. It was built to replace the late-Romanesque church that was destroyed by a devastating earthquake.

ZÜRICH
CULTURED, RICH
AND SEVERE

If Bern is the political capital of Switzerland, Zürich is its commercial and financial capital. Bahnofstrasse and Paradeplatz are the symbols of a Swiss economic market that manages, in its entirety, almost a third of the world's financial worth. A cosmopolitan city, Zürich is a European capital that has welcomed intellectuals, artists, politicians, and scientists from every nation. The Federal Polytechnic Institute, founded in 1864, enjoys great international fame, and its teachers and researchers have won a number of Nobel prizes.

The region around the Lake of Zürich and the Limmat River was already fortified during Roman times. The Gallo-Roman city of Turicium grew at the foot of the castle situated on Lindenhof Hill. In the Middle Ages, a prosperous city developed on the banks of the Limmat. It enjoyed imperial privileges, and the Holy Roman Emperor, when he visited the city, stayed in a palace built on the Lindenhof. At that time, the Fraumünster, a convent founded in 853, and the Grossmünster, a monastery erected in the 12th century upon the ruins of a previous church, were the most notable landmarks.

The early grant of rights to artisans and guilds in the 13th century boosted trade and helped Zürich build its wealth, thereby opening the floodgates to vast cultural development. In 1351, the city joined the League of the Swiss Cantons, in which it immediately assumed a leading role. The Protestant Reformation found the city highly receptive because of the presence of Ulrich Zwingli. His warrior-like fervor made Zürich the crowning glory of the Swiss-German Protestant movement. The Reformation did not favor cul-

93 top right
The monument to
Alfred Escher, which
stands in front of
the train station,
commemorates
one of the city's
most illustrious and
dynamic figures.
Escher had a decisive
role in the creation
of the Federal
Polytechnic Institute,
Crédit Suisse, and
the St. Gotthard
Railway.

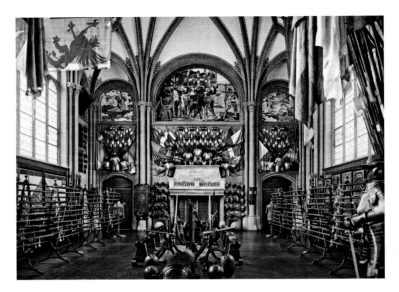

94 top left The Landesmuseum has a million objects, paintings, and "rooms" from pre-history to modern times on display, all from within the region of the present-day Confederation. With the creation of the museum, in 1898, Switzerland wanted to pay tribute to the new federal state.

94 top center Zürich's historic center is quite picturesque, with its colorfully painted houses and its towers that recall the city's long history; it was one of the first to join the Helvetic Confederation.

94 top right The Fraumünster was founded as a convent in 853 by Ludwig of Germany, and enjoyed special privileges until 1524: the nuns, who in fact asserted their lordship over the city, had the right to market dues and to coin money.

94-95 The Grossmünster, with its two giant towers, is in some ways a symbol of the Protestant-reformed city. Built between the 11th and 12th centuries, it dominates the Limmat River with its own massiveness and that of its two giant towers. Traces of remarkable frescoes and paintings can be seen in the choir and the crypt.

95 The Fraumünster, with its spire-like bell tower, is one of the city's most important sights. Inside are stained-glass windows by Marc Chagall, which illustrate about twenty scenes from the Old and New Testaments.

ture; however, manufacturing activities took advantage of the asylum offered to numerous French and Italian Protestant refugees. Culture regained its stride in the 18th century, thanks to European individuals of the caliber of the artist Karl Bodmer, the poet and physiognomist Johann Kaspar Lavater, and the pedagogue Heinrich Pestalozzi. To Zürich's credit, it had faith in the liberal upper class well before other European cities did: in the 19th century, big insurance and financial companies were established that planned extensive construction projects. The inauguration (in 1860) of Credit Suisse and the Northeast Railway, beginning with the Gotthardbahn, the railroad line, and the St. Gotthard Tunnel, is due to Alfred Escher. Two clearly identifiable cores can still be seen in the Old City: the Grossmünster, a basilica from the 12th century on the right bank of the Limmat where Zwingli preached, and the 9th century Fraumünster, on the left bank of the river, connected to the convent for women, built in 853.

Modern Zürich took shape after the demolition of the bastions and the city's internal fortifications at the end of the 19th century, which made it possible to create new spaces and business districts, such as the area around the Central Station and Bahnofstrasse.

Zürich has always enjoyed a cultural life of the highest level. At the beginning of the 20th century, Hugo Ball, Jean Arp, Tristan Tzara and other gifted avant-garde figures gave birth to the Dada Movement at the Cabaret Voltaire. Close to the Polytechnic Institute and the University precinct is the Kunsthaus, a fine-arts museum in Art-Deco style designed by Karl Mozer, as well as the Opera, and the old Corso Theater. The city's numerous private and public collections exhibit works by the most important Swiss painters and sculptors (Anker, Hodler, Vallotton, Alberto Giacometti and others), not to mention great masters of the figurative arts from around the world, with particular emphasis on those of the 20th century. The Landesmuseum exhibits a vast collection of objects illustrating early human settlements in Switzerland and the associated material culture, as well as the traditions and customs of the country over the centuries. In nearby Winterthur, the Oskar Reinhart Museum displays a number masterpiece paintings.

96 top A rich industrial and financial capital, Zürich has the means to erect modern, well-crafted monuments, like the two towers of the Schaumburg, for example, which face and reflect each other.

96 center The people of Zürich love to enjoy the lake and the beauty of nature, above all in summer. The shores of the lake are embellished with parks, lawns, and blooming flowerbeds that delight those who love sports and recreational walking.

96 bottom In front of the traditional façade and decorative roofs of the Tibetan Center, among the best-known and most popular in Europe, is large lawn where young people love to gather, read, or enjoy sunshine during the summer.

96-97 The powerful cement arches of the underground passages in Stadelhofen Station, designed by the Spanish architect Santiago Calatrava, support the upper floor, which carries the railroad tracks.

98 top The St. Gallen
Library, known
throughout the world,
includes the most
beautiful Rococo-style
hall in Switzerland.
The Library has
150,000 books and
over 2,000 medieval
codices, some of
inestimable value,
which can be viewed
and studied.

ST. GALLEN
ORA ET LABORA

99 top left
St. Gallen's baroque
cathedral, with two
towers and a nave
with two side aisles,
was built between
1755 and 1766.
It stands in a vast
clearing in the
middle of an area
once occupied by the
Benedictine abbey.

99 top right
The cathedral's
Baroque interior is
full of decorations,
stuccoes, and frescoes
(on the vaults). The
wooden pulpit, on
which the symbols of
the Four Evangelists
are carved, and the
imposing organ are
extremely valuable.

The city, which is located southeast of Lake Constance, owes its origins to the hermitage built by the monk St. Gallen in 612 during the wave of the continent's Christianization by the Irish monks of St. Columba. In, on the site of the hermitage, St. Otmar founded a true monastery that was enlarged a century later. The urban center gradually grew around the abbey, and for several centuries depended almost completely upon the establishment, which had become one of the main centers of intellectual and religious teaching in Europe.

The library at St. Gallen is one of the most extraordinary in the world. It contains about 150,000 volumes, among which are numerous Irish manuscripts from the 7th to the 12th century and 1,650 incunabula. The most beautiful or rare volumes (illuminated psalm books, the Carolingian map of the abbey, and scrolls) can be admired behind display windows, enhanced by gorgeous carved wooden frames and tall columns. The tradition of embroidery and handmade textiles, which experienced a true explosion on an international scale in the 19th century, dates back to the medieval era, the time when linen was woven in the monasteries and workshops of the city.

98 bottom On the pediment of the cathedral's eastern façade, a bas-relief of the Coronation of the Virgin Mary stands out, a 1933 reconstruction of an original 18th-century work by Joseph Anton Feuchtmayer.

98-99 The Abbey of St. Gallen's huge complex of buildings dates back to the 17th and 18th centuries. Today it houses both the bishop's offices and the cantonal government.

101 top left In the historic center of St. Gallen, the projecting windows called Erker *are typical constructions which often rise up to the fourth floor. The lower margin had to be sufficiently high to allow a loaded haycart to pass under the projection.*

101 top center The little towers of the Erker, *with one or two floors, in wood but also in stone, have variable forms: one-floor cylinders that rise up to the height of the roof or parallelepipeds with only one level.*

101 top right Visitors looking for old workshops happily pause before display windows decorated with laces and needlepoint work. Taverns take advantage of the extensive pedestrian zone to also serve customers sitting outside.

100 top and 100-101 St. Gallen's historic city center boasts gorgeous aristocratic homes, dating from the 16th to the 18th centuries, featuring painted wooden frames, ornaments, and gabled roofs with dormer windows.

100 center The balconies of the projecting windows are often richly decorated, with scenes featuring allegorical or symbolic figures dating back to the Middle Ages.

100 bottom Strolling through the Old City, a searching eye will discover frescoed façades and balconies decorated with big bouquets of flowers, not to mention the unmistakable projecting windows.

LA CHAUX-DE-FONDS AS PRECISE AS A SWISS WATCH

102-103 La Chaux-de-Fonds is in some ways a unique entity. Instead of losing population as did the majority of the regions where the climate is particularly harsh, it became a city thanks to the ingenuity of an artisan who, having invented the wrist watch, attracted many thousands of precision mechanics and goldsmiths to its neighborhoods. The city's structure is emblematic of the emancipated ideals of the working class in fashion during the second half of the 19th and the early 20th centuries: decent housing for everyone, equal even down to the height of the buildings, and direct routes from homes to the factories.

La Chaux-de-Fonds, situated at an altitude of 3200 feet in the Neuchâtel Mountains of the Jura, was almost completely destroyed by fire in 1794. The rebuilding of the city in keeping with a design by Perret-Gentil was begun immediately, and was completed in 1835 by Charles-Henri Junod.

Today La Chaux-de-Fonds is the capital of the Swiss watch industry. Thanks to the genius and enterprising spirit of Daniel Jean-Richard and of the young artists he instructed in the art of clockmaking, the new industry spread during the 18th century throughout the Neuchâtel Mountains and the Jura region. The watch industry, which in the meantime had conquered the entire world, becoming one of the feathers in the cap of the "Made in Switzerland" label, established itself – besides in La Chaux-de-Fonds – in the cities of Le Locle (in the Vallée de Joux), Neuchâtel, and in neighboring Bienne. The International Watchmaking Museum in La Chaux-de-Fonds offers visitors an exhibition of the instruments used by man to tell time from ancient eras up until today. La Chaux-de-Fonds, the city of Art Nouveau, was the birthplace of the automobile manufacturer Louis Chevrolet, the writer Blaise Cendrars, and the great 20th-century architect Charles Edouard Jeanneret, known as Le Corbusier.

103 The watchmaking museum makes it possible for visitors to take an extraordinary journey among the instruments used to measure time: wristwatches, watch hands, pendulums, and carillons, made from a variety of materials, from the simplest to the most artistic and expensive.

104-105 Lucerne is
a tourist destination,
with its ancient
monuments,
walkways along the
River Reuss and
around the lake, and
museums. Overall, it
features a pre-alpine
landscape of a rare
beauty.

LUCERNE
WHERE THE LAKES MIRROR THE ALPS

105 top left The Jesuits
left deep marks on the
history of the city of
Lucerne and that
of the Helvetic
Confederation, both
from an educational
and political point of
view. Visible on the left
of the photo is church
that the Jesuit order
built in 1699 on the
banks of the Reuss.

*104 top Lucerne
may well be the most
charming of the
Swiss cities. Along
the road flanking
the river, crossed
by the Kapellbrücke,
the perfectly
preserved façades,
roofs, and towers
of the old city come
one after the other.*

*104 bottom Visible in
the background is the
Hofkirche, a cathedral
dedicated to Saint
Leodegar. It features
two elegant late-
Gothic bell-towers,
between which a 17th-
century façade was
built, dating to 1639,
the same year as the
gorgeous organ inside.*

The history of Lucerne is closely tied to its geographical location and to its relations with the ancient cantons of Uri, Schwyz, and Unterwalden. The city, which in 1291 the Abbot of Murbach ceded to Rudolf I of Hapsburg, had to wait until 1332 to gain its independence, upon which it joined the Confederation.

Located at the northwestern end of the "Lake of the Four Cantons," Lucerne had become a center of trade for goods in transit between Flanders and Italy, important for the cantons of the early league. With the opening of the St. Gotthard Pass by the people of the Uri Canton, trade at the fairs in Lombardy began to increase, and all of Switzerland started to profit. Within a few decades, the city – strong with the support of the league and a treaty between farmers and noble families – was able to defeat the Hapsburgs in the memorable battle of Sempach (1386). Expanding within its city walls, on the banks of the River Reuss, Lucerne has maintained its medieval layout. Its fortifications are still highly visible: the Mühletor, the walls of the Mussegg, and on the banks of the river, the Wasserturm and the lovely wooden bridge of Kapellbrücke (the oldest wooden bridge in Europe, built in 1300). The city's famous 19th-century monument of the lion symbolically represents the Swiss Guard's vain attempt on 10 August 1792 to defend the Tuileries, where Louis XVI and his family were residing as the French Revolution grew in fury.

Lucerne, along with Fribourg, remained a great bastion of Catholicism

105 top right Some buildings in Lucerne present colorful old frescoes commissioned by families or guilds to show off their wealth. More recent creations include these masks and Carnival figures on the façade of Restaurant Fritschi.

106 top left Lucerne boasts a long tradition of figurative arts, theater, and musical performance. Contemporary artists of repute have contributed to uphold this reputation with highly modern productions.

106 center left This nighttime panorama is truly unique and unmistakable: the Kapellbrücke, the medieval wooden bridge, and the Wasserturm, the tower on the River Reuss, both brightly lit, reflected in the waters of the river.

106 bottom left The Lucerne station, a railroad hub of primary importance in Switzerland, is a monumental building renovated in the recent past.

106 bottom right The writer Mark Twain, passing through Lucerne, described the

monument of the dying lion as the most tragic and moving piece of rock in the world.

106-107 The Reuss originates from the St. Gotthard massif and rushes into the Lake of the Four Cantons, after having flowed through the original Swiss cantons to then

flow out, torrentially, at the level of Lucerne.

107 top left Numerous historic hotels are reflected in the waters of Lake Lucerne. The Palace Hotel, like many others, attests to the extraordinary tourist boom Lucerne

experienced in the 19th and early 20th centuries.

107 top right A chapel was built into the Spreuerbrücke, a 15th-century wooden bridge. The famous Dance of Death, painted by Kaspar Meglinger, attracts visitors from around the world.

during the Reformation and also during the civil war of Sonderbund in 1847, which divided the cantons. The Jesuit order exerted a powerful influence in Lucerne and played a significant role in political events until their expulsion from Switzerland. The Jesuit church of San Francesco Saverio is noteworthy as the first great Swiss Baroque church.

In the 19th century, Lucerne became an obligatory stop for tourists, particularly for those from England. During this period, it expanded its hotel industry, in the historic center, on the banks of the lake, and at the base of the surrounding peaks, starting with Mt. Pilatus.

108 top left The castle housing the episcopal offices – a mighty but elegant construction renovated in the 18th century – is reached by passing through the tower door.

108 top right The church of St. Martin dates back to the 8th century but was touched up a few centuries later according to the canons of late-Gothic style. In it, early-20th-century stained glass windows can be admired.

108-109 Chur is an ancient city. The Romans gave it the name of Curia Rhaetorum, from which comes the modern-day name. Churches and towers attest to its political and religious role in the Middle Ages.

109 top Chur has
been an episcopal seat
since the year 450.
The cathedral – with
a nave and two side
aisles, built between
the 12th and 13th
centuries in
Romanesque and
Gothic style –
represents the city's
ancient heart.
The frescoes and the
Gothic triptych in
the choir are gorgeous.

CHUR
THE FREE CITY
OF THE THREE LEAGUES

In Roman times, Chur was the capital of an extensive region known as "Rhaetia Prima." The city, located in the Rhine Valley but far from the river, was a bishop's seat as early as the end of the 5th century. Though Chur lacked the strategic and religious importance of the abbey of Disentis (8th century), located close to the Lukmanier Pass, by the 16th century it had become the political, religious, and administrative hub of the Rhaetian region. The population were originally speakers of a Rhaeto-Romansch language, but the region was Germanized by the Walser peoples from the Valais, who began settling there in the 13th century.

Rhaetia had been part of the Holy Roman Empire since the 9th century, and the process of separation from the Empire pushed local communities to form leagues. Thus were born the League of God's House (in 1367), the Grey League (1395), and the League of the Ten Jurisdictions (1436), which formed, from 1524 until the founding of the Helvetian Republic in 1798, the "Free State of the Three Leagues." The leagues stabilized the Rhaetian territory and even attempted to enact a policy of expansion, quickly annexing the Valtellina region. Pressure from Austrian Lombardy (and meddling by other Swiss cantons) when the nations that had defeated Napoleon met at the Congress of Vienna prevented the delegates from assigning the territory of the Valtellina to the Grisons and Italian-speaking Switzerland.

Several Italian-language regions are part of the Grisons Canton: the Val Bregaglia, the Val Poschiavo, and the Calanca and Mesolcina valleys, bordering on Ticino Canton. As a result, in the county seat of Chur, three languages are spoken: German, Romansch, and Italian, which is taught in the schools.

The city of Chur is overlooked by the rocky face of the Calanda (9200 ft) but it is open to the north in the direction of the Rhine and to the south toward the valleys and passes leading to the famous winter resorts of Lenzerheide, Arosa, Davos, and St. Moritz.

109 bottom Chur's historic center, an area enclosed in an almost perfect half-circle, has been well conserved and has been systematically restored over recent years.

FRIBOURG
WHERE THE
LANGUAGES MEET

111 top left The old
medieval houses, built
close to each other,
flank Lausanne
Street and the
Grande Rue, the
main street, which
descends towards
Zähringen Bridge
and the lower city
from the town hall.

This charming city lies in a region that has been inhabited since ancient times and which enjoyed significant importance during the Roman era. The powerful family of Zähringen founded Fribourg, and also Freiburg (the same name in variant dialect) in the state of Baden-Württemberg in southwestern Germany. Fribourg lies along a wide bend in the Sarine. In its early period, the city was enclosed by borders dug into the *molasse* rock, but in the medieval period imposing fortifications were built, of which more than a mile of city wall and 14 defensive towers are still standing. Today, the visitor can enjoy Gothic-style St. Nicholas Cathedral and the handsome City Hall, which features a fine clock tower. From these two buildings, historic streets flanked by well preserved late medieval houses lead down toward the lower city with its artisan neighborhoods, dominated by im-

posing fortifications, where wool was produced and skins were tanned. In the late-Middle Ages, the fertile pasture lands adjoining Fribourg were the home of pig and cattle raising, and the processing and marketing of meat products flourished. Industrial-scale production of cheese and dairy products is still highly developed, not only in the Gruyère area – the home of the world-famous cheese – but throughout the region. In modern times, because of the abundant and excellent milk produced in the area, such firms as Villars and Nestlé have established chocolate factories in the city and nearby Broc.

Fribourg has a rich religious history. After the bishop's see had been established, religious orders joined the numerous monasteries, of which the Cistercian house of Hauterive is noteworthy. During the Reformation, Fribourg became a bastion of Catholicism. The university, founded at the end of the 19th century by Georges Phyton, has a solid tradition in the teaching of theology, thanks to the presence of an important Dominican school. It is also known for its faculties of economics, the sciences, and Italian literature. This last faculty was home to Gianfranco Contini, as well as other distinguished scholars.

110 The oldest part of Fribourg is dominated by the Gothic cathedral of St. Nicholas, with its tall tower crowned by spires. The 15th-century portal is called "the Portal of the Apostles" and the gable features a depiction of the Day of Judgment.

110-111 The neighborhoods in the old city, which gradually descend toward the river following the terrain step by step, are connected to each other by old wooden bridges in the lower city and big bridges in the upper city, some of which were once suspension bridges.

111 top right Fribourg's Town Hall, which is also the seat of the cantonal Parliament, looks onto a medieval square creating the perfect setting for a centenary linden tree. The tree commemorates the marathon a soldier ran to alert the authorities of Fribourg of the victory of the Swiss against the Burgundians in the battle in nearby Morat.

*112 top left Sion
is the capital of the
Valais Canton. It is
the headquarters of
the government and
cantonal parliament,
the bishopric, and many
prosperous industries.*

*112 top right The
Town Hall was built
in the 17th century.
The façade is dominated
by a tower with an
astrological clock.
Its atrium contains
precious inscriptions
from the Roman and
early Christian eras.*

SION
A FORTRESS AMONG
THE VINEYARDS

*112-113 Built
on the banks of the
Rhône and on the
hills upon which sit
the castles of Valère
and Tourbillon, the
city is surrounded
by vineyards and
the lovely frame
of the alpine chain.*

*113 top The
cathedral of Notre
Dame de Sion, located
in the historic center
at the foot of the
castles, is dedicated to
the Virgin Mary and
houses many treasures*

*of great value,
including rare
volumes and ancient
incunabula.*

*113 bottom Located
on top of one of Sion's
hills, the cathedral-
castle of Valère was
built in the 12th
century and served
as the residence of
the canons of the
cathedral's chapter
until the French
Revolution. Today, it
is one of Switzerland's
oldest historical
museums.*

After ancient Octodurus (Martigny), Sedunum (Sion) was the main Roman settlement in the Valaisian region. Martigny, located at the approaches to the Great St. Bernard Pass, became the administrative center of the Roman province of the Pennine Alps. The region was thereafter occupied by the Burgundians and then the Franks before being incorporated into the Holy Roman Empire.

At the beginning of the 11th century, the Burgundian king Rudolf III gave the Valais to the bishopric of Sion, whose spiritual leaders had resided in the city since the 6th century. The figure of the Prince-bishop had a determining effect on the political history of the Valais Canton and the city, as demonstrated by the complex of the Church of Our Lady of Valère, at the top of the hill overlooking Sion. Valère was a fortified citadel containing the church (also fortified, with a bell-tower that used to serve as the donjon) and some residential buildings. After the defeat of Napoleon, the allies, meeting in the Congress of Vienna, considered the future status of a number of previously French-dominated territories and sanctioned the entry of the Valais into the Helvetic Confederation. With this political change, Sion became the county seat of the new canton. Sion is not only the administrative and political center but also the economic center of a canton that derives much of its income from viticulture and tourism. The rich historic and cultural past of Sion is reconstructed in the city's museums. In addition, neighboring Martigny is home to the Gallo-Roman Museum, to the Pierre Gianadda Foundation with its changing series of exhibitions, and to other venues that features noteworthy exhibits of great modern painting.

This region of the Rhône valley has a rich mix of cultures and traditions; it also divides into two distinctly different linguistic areas. People in the Upper Valais speak German. This results from an event that occurred in the Middle Ages. The Walsers of Germany migrated to the southern slopes of the Alps, to Ossola and Formazza, to the Bernese and Grisons Alps, bringing with them their language along with their customs and traditions. The charm of the Valais' challenging mountains and the lateral valleys has been praised by numerous writers, among whom Charles Ferdinand Ramuz stands out.

LAUSANNE
CITY OF OLYMPIC CALM

Lausanne combines a historic past with an important modern role. The city, which developed from an early Roman settlement, occupies a magnificent hill-side site on Lake Geneva's northern shore. The Cathedral of Notre Dame – the most beautiful Gothic building in Switzerland – was consecrated in the 1270s by Pope Gregory X in the presence of Rudolf I of Hapsburg; it is now used for Protestant worship because of the city's decision to embrace the Reformation. In the 18th century, Lausanne fell under the charm of the Enlightenment. Voltaire staged his play *Zadig* in the city, and Sainte-Beuve gave the lectures that he later published as *Port-Royal*, his work on the religious movement known as Jansenism that deeply affected 17th-century France.

Today Lausanne is renowned as the headquarters of the International Olympic Committee (ICO), founded in 1894 by Pierre de Coubertin, and the Olympic Museum located in the Ouchy neighborhood. The Orchestra of French-speaking Switzerland enjoys great prestige, and Maurice Béjart chose the city to be the home for his dance troupe. Lausanne is also the location of the State Polytechnic Institute and the Federal Court, the highest court in the Swiss Confederation.

115 top right
The town hall of Lausanne la Palud was built in 1672 on the grounds of a earlier structure and enlarged in the 18th and 19th centuries. A clock-tower looms over the Renaissance-style façade.

116 top The cathedral, built between 1170 and 1215 on the city's high ground, and dominated by an imposing spire, is a gorgeous Gothic monument in the French and Anglo-Norman style.

116-117 A lake town, Lausanne enjoys a mild climate that attracts numerous visitors and supports a large accommodation industry. The lake shore in the Ouchy area is embellished by plants and flowers.

117 top The city is the headquarters of the International Olympic Committee and contains the Olympic Museum, opened in 1993. Visiting it makes it possible to relive magic moments in sports, framed in their historical, political, cultural, and scientific contexts.

117 center The cathedral's entrances feature Gothic decorations with sculptural works in molasse rock. The most important one is the rose window in the south transept, featuring magnificent stained glass.

117 bottom The big, main nave with Gothic-arch vaults is a work by Jean Cotereel. The apse contains precious stained-glass windows. The eastern, and older, part of the building features Romanesque-style architectural elements.

GENEVA
AN INTERNATIONAL SOUL

Today Geneva is often thought of as just a modern "headquarters" city. The United Nations and some two hundred or so multinational organizations, including the International Committee of the Red Cross, the International Labor Office, and the World Trade Organization have their European headquarters in the city on the lake. But Geneva has thousands of years of history that should not be forgotten. The region was inhabited as early as the Neolithic era; given its geographical location it was incorporated into the Roman Empire, which event occurred in the 2nd century B.C. Centuries later, in 1033, Geneva became incorporated into the Holy Roman Empire as an imperial and episcopal city. Geneva's coat-of-arms, featuring half an eagle and golden keys, recalls part of its historical origins. Geneva's historic center developed over the ruins of the Roman city, upon which the medieval nucleus is overlaid. The city's major church, St. Peter's Cathedral, was built at the end of the 12th century on the site of earlier Romanesque basilicas. Close to the cathedral stands the Temple of the Auditorium, where Calvin and John Knox, the two champions of the Reformation, preached their doctrines.

Geneva's strategic geographical position at the point where the Rhône flows out of Lake Geneva has meant that it has had to defend itself from the expansionist appetites of the house of Savoy. In the 16th century, Geneva signed its first treaty with the Swiss League, but it had to wait three centuries (1815) before it could enter into the Confederation, a welcome accession to freedom for a city that had been annexed by France in 1789 and under her domination until 1813. The city was deeply affected by the Reformation and, in

118 bottom *Watchmaking – a Swiss tradition of precision micro-engineering, which has one of its capitals in Geneva – is transformed into a naturalistic attraction in the famous flower-clock in the Jardin Anglais.*

118-119 International Geneva, with its famous hotels and bridges, marks the gulf of Lake Geneva with the unmistakable Jet d'eau, at the point where the Rhône flows out to continue on its course through nearby France.

119 top The Pont du Mont Blanc, in the heart of the city center, crosses the Rhône and connects the museum quarter with that of the luxurious hotels and inns.

120 top left St. Peter's Cathedral has a Romanesque structure onto which Gothic elements were grafted. A bastion of Catholicism until the 15th century, it became a pulpit for the Reformation. John Calvin and John Knox preached there. A highly interesting archaeological site has been excavated under the cathedral.

particular, by the presence of Calvin, who transformed it into "Reformed Rome," the center of Protestant radicalism. Though this situation damaged Roman Catholics, French Protestant refugees greatly benefitted since from the 17th century onward they had set up flourishing industrial and banking businesses there. In the 18th century, the city attracted many leading proponents of the Enlightenment, of whom Voltaire was the most notable. Cultural debate flourished wth the arrival of Rousseau and Madame de Staël. The tradition of higher education is deeply engrained in the city, which has distinguished itself in the pedagogical sciences, with Piaget, and linguistic studies with de Saussure.

In the sciences, Geneva is famous as the home of the European Center for Nuclear Research (CERN). It is distinguished as the headquarters of International Committee of the Red Cross, and for the Geneva Convention, a foundation document in efforts to ensure and to monitor human rights.

121 top Geneva is the third most important Swiss financial market (Zürich is the first, Lugano the second). Besides the large credit institutions, it hosts numerous medium-sized, family-owned private banks.

121 bottom Geneva, the headquarters of the International Committee of the Red Cross (founded by Henry Dunant, a son of the city), is also the "city guardian" of the Geneva conventions, on which the principles of international human rights are based.

122-123 *The bell-tower of the church of S. Lorenzo dominates the city and Lake Lugano. In the background are the slopes of Mount Bré and, on the other side of the lake, Italy's Lanzo d'Intelvi mountains.*

LUGANO
THE GATEWAY TO THE MEDITERRANEAN

Today Lugano is Switzerland's third most important financial center, the main economic hub of Italian-speaking Switzerland, and a noteworthy international tourist destination. But it had to struggle for this status. During the Middle Ages Lugano's history was marked by territorial wars between Como and Milan. In 1512, after a brief period under French domination, troops of the Swiss Confederation conquered the city and its hinterlands and made it a ward of the Swiss cantons. After three centuries of this dependent status, it was liberated on February 15, 1798, thanks to a popular uprising that followed a failed attempt to annex it to the nearby Cisalpine Republic. This state was the short-lived entity, centered on the River Po valley, that Napoleon had created after his victories in northern Italy.

Lugano's handsome architectural heritage includes the Romanesque cathedral of San Lorenzo, with its beautiful Renaissance façade, and the church of Santa Maria degli Angioli, built at the end of the 15th century and frescoed by Bernardino Luini. The illustrious Comacine and Compagnon masters, and the great Francesco Castelli di Bissone (known as il Borromini) also left their mark on Lugano. The city has some noteworthy modern buildings, several by the architect Mario Botta, including his renowned church of Santa Maria degli Angeli on Mount Tamaro. In the early 19th century Lugano distinguished itself for its progressive political policies and publications. During the Risorgimento era, the city welcomed numerous illustrious Italian exiles who contributed to enlivening political discussion; among them was the liberal federalist Carlo Cattaneo, to whom

a museum in Castagnola is dedicated. During the first half of the 20th century, the city was also a haven for numerous exiled Italians, fleeing Fascism and war. In 1996 the Università della Svizzera Italiana was established as a new academic center, specializing in finance, the communication sciences, computer science, and architecture.

Lake Lugano and its picturesque countryside has enthralled artists and writers; among the best known is Herman Hesse, who spent the last years of his life painting and writing in nearby Montagnola.

WHEN TRADITION
IS A CHOICE

125 top right The first tossing match of the Unspunnen Stone (named for the field at Interlaken where it was held) took place on 17 August 1805, during the period of a strong search for national identity after occupation by Napoleon's troops.

124 bottom In the Landsgemeinde today, votes are cast by raising an orange card in the air. Until a few decades ago, voting was restricted to men only, who voted by lifting their sword.

124-125 In Glarus, people still vote in Zaunplatz, the town's main square. Living symbols of direct Swiss democracy, the Landsgemeinde are an ancient form of public expression of an individual's vote on all issues regarding not only the local but the national community as well.

125 top left During Lucerne's Alpine Festival, featuring Swiss wrestling, the "house special" – apart from the wrestling matches – is still tossing the so-called Unspunnen Stone, weighing about 175 pounds.

The Swiss feel different from others, as if precise cultural characteristics existed to bind them together. Though it may be true that confederate political bonds have strengthened over the centuries, big differences in language, culture, and traditions still exist between the nation's inhabitants. The Latin substratum has been able to stay alive and develop in the regions west of the River Sarine, south of the Alps, and in the Rhaeto-Romansch valleys of the Grisons. Germanization has, on the other hand, prevailed north of the Alps, markedly so in the northeastern region and in large measure also in the Grisons. In the cantons straddling the Sarine River – but also in the Valais populated by Walser peoples – both French and German is spoken. In the Grisons, German, Romansch, and Italian are spoken. In the Ticino Canton, the common language is Italian.

Today in Switzerland, there are still three official languages: German (spoken by the majority), French, and Italian. Romansch is the fourth national language but it is now spoken only by a small minority in the Grisons. In truth, German is not really the language spoken: in German-speaking Switzerland, everyone speaks the local dialect, even the upper classes. As for religious borders, they do not correspond to the linguistic ones: central and southern Switzerland and the Fribourg Canton and the Valais Canton are predominantly Catholic. In the rest of the territory (above all in the big cities), the majority of the population is Protestant or equally divided between the two main sects of the Christian religion.

On 1 August 1891, for the first time and by decision of the federal government, the birth of the Helvetic Confederation – 600 years earlier – was solemnly celebrated.

This was done to the chiming of bells and with bonfires lit on all the hills of the country. The first national Helvetic tradition is, in fact, that of the bonfires, still widely maintained today during August 1 celebrations, to which fireworks have been gradually added in numerous Swiss towns and cities. By the beginning of the 19th century, holidays had been added to safeguard ancient patriotic traditions. In 1805, celebrations of the mountain shepherds were inaugurated at Unspunnen, the focal point of which is the pitching of a giant stone known as the Stone of Unspunnen. The Sechseläuten celebrations in Zürich (still strictly limited to men) and the Gansabhauet in Sursee, near Lucerne, are clear expressions of the importance of civil society on institutions in Switzerland.

The calendar of national holidays, which was established in 1824, expresses the pride of a mercenary people who for centuries trudged across fields of battle throughout Europe and for whom the institution of military exercises naturally inclines to use arms. The ritual of these exercises was inspired by the one created in France after the Revolution and imported into Switzerland by the Helvetian Republic in 1798. Cannon shots and soldiers parading to the beat of drums in 18th-century uniforms at dawn still open the August 1 commemorations in several Swiss locations. On the other hand, every soldier-citizen, until the age of 40 years old, owns a weapon and must fire, once a year, the so-called "obligatory shot" at communal stands set up for that purpose. The ancient patriotic customs play an im-

126 Among Switzerland's popular festivals, Zürich's spring celebration of Sechseläuten is among the most famous and well-liked. Even children wear traditional clothing and wrap crowns of flowers around their heads.

127 top Flames envelop the so-called Boegg, a big doll that at Zürich's Sechseläuten symbolizes the passing of spring. When the head pops off the body, it means that summer has arrived under the most auspicious circumstances.

127 bottom left In Sursee, in the Lucerne Canton, people in costumes parade during the Gansabhauet Festival, carrying geese in their arms. The sun mask (visible bottom right) is worn during the course of the celebrations.

127 bottom right During the Sechseläuten parade, characters of all kinds parade, dressed in the gaudiest traditional outfits or in old-fashioned clothes. There are also many bands playing.

portant role in social cohesion and reached their height in the first half of the 20th century, during the period of the so-called "spiritual resistance" of Switzerland to the Nazi-Fascist threat. Several associations founded at the beginning of the 20th century to maintain and safeguard the Helvetian cultural heritage have actively done so.

In some cantons, traditions and political life are perfectly matched, though separated by centuries, in the Landsgemeinde, the open-air popular assemblies where the whole political community gathers in large squares to elect their representatives and to vote, by raising their hands, on political issues subject to popu-

lar ruling. This archaic system still governs the small half-cantons of Inner Appenzell and Outer Appenzell, and the cantons of Obwald, and Nidwald, and Glarus. On the last Sunday of April, the Landsgemeinde of the two half cantons of Appenzell and Unterwalden gather. The citizens of Glarus meet on the first Sunday in May. Such open-air assemblies also exist, albeit with fewer duties to fulfill, in some districts of the Grisons and Schwyz, not to mention in a few guilds in central Switzerland. In earlier times, men voted with a sword, and women were excluded. Only in the last few decades have women been able to exercise their right to vote in the Landsgemeinde.

128 top The big bells on Swiss cows emit a typical sound, which echoes from pasture to pasture, from valley to valley. The prettiest ones are hung on the façades of farmhouses or barns.

128-129 The alpenhorn, the super-long wooden instrument, resting against the ground and played by mountain people dressed in their typical clothing, is Switzerland's impressive national instrument.

Like a solemn frame to the patriotic traditions of the Swiss Alps, there are a few typical popular songs, the so-called "yodels," and the giant horns of the Alps – the national Swiss instruments. Yodeling is a melodious form of singing in falsetto that is found, in its various forms, in the mountain cantons of Appenzell, Toggenburg, the Bernese Oberland, and Gruyère. It is essentially a song-prayer of cowherds. It is also known as a call-chant directed at the beasts at pasture or during milking. Of ancient origin, it draws upon the ritual-magic singing of the shepherds. The sound is that of litanies or psalms. The yodelers' duets and choral chants are also found in the Muota and Weggis valleys. The alpine horn is an instrument more than seven feet long and curved at the end: it is balanced against the ground and is played at popular festivals by dairymen *(armaillis)* dressed in a traditional grey-blue outfit decorated with edelweiss. Playing the horn requires immense lung capacity. Its sound, languid and deep, has made an impression on great composers like Brahms. Its curve is the natural shape of a fir tree that has grown crooked under the weight of snow on a slope.

Other instruments typical of the pastoral culture are the cowbells and harness bells that adorn the collar on cows, especially on the ascent up the mountain to the high summer pastures and on the return. The long procession of cows with their horns decorated with flowers and little flags as though at a party, which climb up the mountain from the plain at the be-

129 top Once a year, in the Valais village of Aproz, the most vigorous of the Hérens cows fight each other before a large crowd. This bovine breed is particularly strong and individuals will fight for dominance within the herd.

129 bottom In Vevey, during the grape-harvest festival, cows are adorned with crowns of grapes and flowers, not to mention large bells decorated with phrases commemorating the event.

ginning of summer, to the beat of their large decorated bells, represent one of the most widespread traditions in alpine areas. Depending on the region, the processions are called *poja* or *majen*. In the Valais, in Aproz, the fighting cows of the Hérens breed compete in battles to obtain the title of Queen of the Meadow; the events are known as the *combat des reines*. Today, television and tourism convey the ancient charm of these alpine customs, but a good part of these traditions are still a spontaneous and vibrant expression of the Swiss social conscience.

130 In the Lötschen Valley, in the German-speaking upper Valais, frightening wooden masks are worn during Carnival. The tradition is ancient, and it is said that anything goes for those wearing masks.

131 top In Appenzell Canton on New Year's Day, the people parade in old-fashioned costumes and masks. The head coverings recall images in miniatures portraying animals and farming scenes.

131 center In the alpine regions and the countryside, ancient traditions survive. Masks are a constant not only at Carnival, and vary from region to region.

131 bottom The Carnival parades in Basel are famous and attract a big audience. Because of the beauty of their costumes, the local masked groups are invited to Carnival parades all over Switzerland.

In the Catholic cantons, large town-sponsored processions (for example, the solemn occasion of the "Fête Dieu," or Corpus Domini, in Fribourg) are an expression of the community's religious and cultural identity. Some religious holidays are particularly rooted in Switzerland and are typical expressions of shared emotions: on Christmas, the bringer of gifts is Saint Nicolao, dressed in the garb of bishops in the Catholic cantons, and under the Germanized name of "Samichlaus" and without the episcopalian traits in Protestant areas. The Christmas tree (imported in the 19th century from Germany) is present throughout the country. Eggs are also part of the Easter tradition in Switzerland, and in several areas communities organize egg hunts.

Of all the rituals tied to the seasons, Carnival is without doubt among the most deeply rooted in Switzerland, especially in Basel and the Loetschental. In fact, at Basel in the 15th century, balls and costume parties were planned even during Lent: the Church had to intervene to prohibit these lively festivities at least during Christmas celebrations. In some Catholic cantons, Carnival still begins today with the Epiphany. In the regions in the Ticino Canton that observe Ambrosian rites, it finishes far later than Ash Wednesday. In certain cantons, strongly influenced by the restrictions of the Reformation (Bern and Geneva), no Carnival tradition exists. In several cities (such as Fribourg), the end of winter is highlighted by costume parties and bonfires at which the old year is burned away. In Basel, as of the 19th century, Carnivalesque celebrations are also expressed through the "Ausspielen," sarcastic parodies of past events, which are then imitated in numerous other places. Basel's Carnival processions are particularly stunning, with Mummentschanz performances. Also worth mentioning are those of Neûchatel and Bellinzona.

In the periphery of the alpine valley of Loetschental, in the upper Valais, a mysterious cult of masks has survived more than in other places in Switzerland. Completely isolated from the rest of the world until the beginning of the last century because of the tall peaks encircling it, the Loetschental has maintained its ancestral customs and a dynamic folkloristic tradition. Religious holidays – and in particular that of Corpus Domini – have an ancient feel, emphasized by their traditional outfits, banners and flags, and unaltered rituals. Acting as the counterpoint to so much religiosity, during Carnival (from February 2 to Ash Wednesday) the custom of the monstrous wooden masks is let loose, inset with witch's teeth, worn by the Tschäggättä, bands of bandits cloaked in furs, which in ancient times ran rampant in the valley. The Tschäggättä Parade is the climax of Loetschental's Carnival.

The majority of country festivals and fairs take place at the end of summer, amd celebrate the completion of harvesting. The festival of the Bénichon in Fribourg is famous, with its typical, rich menu. Originally, these occasions were often combined with costume balls and shooting matches. In Lucerne, this aspect is still present on the occasion of the autumn feast, the Herbstfastnacht, the autumn carnival. From the end of September to the beginning of October, wine festivals and harvest parades take place in the country's winemaking regions, such as Lugano.

132-133 *The so-called* Schwingen, *or Swiss wrestling, is almost a national sport in central and alpine Switzerland. Handsome country men compete during the popular festivals on platforms covered with sand or sand and sawdust.*

132 top left Entire towns in central and alpine Switzerland attend the Schwingen matches. The favorite players are usually young country boys, cheered on by the audience. The winners parade around the village streets wearing a crown of flowers.

132 top right In Swiss wrestling, competitors try to pin their opponents' shoulders to the ground with body feints and, above all, with hard tugs on their adversaries' pants.

133 bottom left The flag-throwing with the Swiss flag or that of the canton is part of the ritual typical of popular festivals., above all in the cantons that live off sheep-herding (central and alpine Switzerland and the Bern and Fribourg cantons).

133 bottom right Shooting is one of the Swiss national sports. Every Swiss soldier-citizen keeps a military rifle in his house until the age of 40 and is expected to practice every year.

Swiss national sports have developed in close relation to the shooting and gymnastic associations that were established at the end of the 19th century as clubs advocating social progress. Shooting competitions are numerous, and in taverns in the country it is common to see trophies on display. In the so-called "ancient cantons" of central Switzerland, crossbow tournaments are still held using the legendary weapon of William Tell. Flag-throwing, the *hornuss* (a hard ball fired from a sort of harquebus and hit with a racket), and Swiss wrestling are very popular sports in these regions. Swiss wrestling is closely tied to farming practices. It takes place in summer, at the end of the harvest, in the setting of a whole-hearted common-man's holiday. Competitors wrestle on circles of sand wearing the typical leather pants and attempt to pin their adversary's shoulders against the ground.

Card games are highly popular in Switzer-land. The first demonstration of card games was given in 1300 in Basel by Johannes von Rheinfelden, a monk. In the 14th century, in this city on the Rhine, people were already playing with decks of cards very similar to those in use today. The stakes at that point were high, to the extent that city authorities had to intervene and impose restrictions and heavy sanctions; playing cards, for example, was prohibited during Mass and at nighttime. The Protestant movement fought hard against what its leaders determined to be a pernicious vice. The most widespread card game in German-speaking Switzerland is *jass*. Evidence of this game was found in Schaffhausen in the 18th century, where it seems to have been introduced by Dutch mercenaries. Newspapers write about *jass* in specially-dedicated columns and television program hosts talk about it on special programs; in addition, a national competition is also held that is extremely popular.

INDEX

Note: c = *caption*

A

Aare, River, 43, 46, 48, 74, 78c, 79
Aarau, 74
Aargau, 18, 20, 21, 29, 30, 79
Abbey, 18c, 98, 98c
Adige, River, 40, 46
Agen, 18
Aigle, 74
Albert II of Hapsburg, 21
Albula Pass, 53
Aletsch Glacier, 43, 43c, 67
Aletschorn, Mt., 53
Alexander of Russia, Czar, 29
Alps, 18, 20, 22, 28c, 37, 40, 43, 43c,
    46, 46c, 48, 54c, 64, 64c, 67, 71c, 72,
    72c, 73c, 74c, 76, 113, 124, 128
Alsace, 20, 87
Altdorf, 20c, 21
America, 8
Andermatt, 41c, 50c, 72, 72c, 73c
Anker, 95
Anniviers, 67
Aosta, 18
Appenzell Canton, 8c, 22, 24, 32, 64,
    127, 128, 131c
Aproz, 129, 129c
Arosa, 109
Arp, Jean, 95
Atlantic Ocean, 46
Auer, Hans Wilhelm, 83, 84c
Augst, 18
Augusta Raurica, 18 (see also Augst)
Australia, 8
Austria, 21, 24, 30, 31, 36c, 37
Autun, 18
Avenches, 110
Aventicum, 18 (see also Avenches)

B

Baden, 40, 74, 74c
Baden-Württemberg, 87
Bakunin, Mikhail Alexandrovich, 30
Ball, Hugo, 95
Bamberg, bishopric of, 74c
Bank of International Settlements, 36c
Basel Canton, 90c
Basel, 20, 22, 24, 27c, 28c, 30, 32, 36c,
    43, 46, 64c, 74, 76, 77, 79, 86-91,
    131, 131c, 133
Béjart, Maurice, 114
Bellinzona, 22, 76, 76c, 131
Bénichon, festival, 131
Bernard, St., of Mentone, 54c
Bern Canton, 30, 53, 67, 79, 133c
Bern, 20, 22, 24, 27, 28, 29, 30c, 31,
    39, 46c, 48, 53, 64, 74, 78c, 79-85,
    92, 131
Bernina Hostel, 54
Bernina Pass, 46, 59c
Bernoulli, Giovanni, 27, 27c, 88
Bibracte, 18
Bienne, 74, 103
Bienne, Lake, 46
Bienne-Morat-Neuchâtel, 64
Birs, River, 64
Bismarck, Otto von, 32
Black Lake, the, 46
Black Sea, 40, 46
Blenio Valley, 22
Bock, Hans, 90c
Bodan, Lake, 40, 46, 48, 64c, 65c (see
    also Constance, Lake)
Bodmer, Karl, 95
Bonaparte, Napoleon, 27c, 28, 29, 54c
Borromeo, St. Carlo, 24

Botta, Mario, 123
Bouchot, François, 28c
Boveri family, the, 74
Brahms, 128
Bré, Mt., 72, 72c
Bregaglia Valley, 43, 109
Bremgarten, 74
Brévine, 64
Brienz, Lake, 46
Brienz, Lake, 74c
Brissago Islands, 72
Broc, 110
Brown family, the, 74
Broye, River, 46
Brugg, 74
Burgdorf, 74, 76
Burgundy, 20, 90c

C

Calanca Valley, 109
Calatrava, Santiago, 97c
Calvin, John, 24, 24c, 118, 120c, 121
Cambrena, 54c
Castagnola, 123
Castelli of Bissone, Francesco (known as
    "il Borromini"), 123
Cattaneo, Carlo, 30, 123
Cendrars, Blaise, 103
Ceresio, Lake, 46, 72, 123c (see also
    Lugano, Lake)
Chagall, Marc, 95c
Champfer, Lake, 59c
Chandolin, 67
Charlemagne, 20
Charles the Bold, duke of Burgundy, 22
Chasseral, Mt., 64
Chevrolet, Louis, 103
Chillon Castle, 76, 77c
Chillon, 20
Chur, 108-109 (see also Curia
    Rhetorum)
Ciba, company, 87
Cisalpine Republic, 123
Columba, St., 18, 98
Como, 123
Como, Lake, 59c
Confederation of the Thirteen Cantons,
    22
Confederation, Helvetic, the, 20c, 21,
    22, 22c, 25, 27, 29, 30, 30c, 32, 35,
    36, 72, 74c, 79, 90c, 92c, 95c, 104,
    104c, 113, 118, 124, 127, 131
Congress of Münster, 24c
Congress of Vienna, 30, 30c, 79, 109, 113
Constance, 46, 74
Constance, Lake, 18, 46, 46c, 64, 65c,
    98 (see also Bodensee)
Contini, Gianfranco, 110
Convention, Stans, 22
Cotereel, Jean, 117c
Council of Basle, 24c, 87
Council of Trent, 24
Crans Montana, 67, 67c
Crédit Suisse, 32
Curaglia, 53c
Curia Rhaetorum, 108c (see also Chur)

D

Dada, 95
Danube River, 8, 40, 46
Davos, 109
De Saussure, Ferdinand 118, 121
De St. Phalle, Niki, 88c
De Travers Valley, 64
Declaration of the Second Helvetian
    Confession, 24
Decoubertin, Pierre, 114
Defense Charter of Wil, 25

Democratic Union of the Center, 39
Dent Blanche, Mt., 53
Diablerets, Mountains, 67
Diavolezza, 59, 59c
Diet of the Swiss Cantons, 27
Disentis Abbey, 109
Doubs, River, 46, 64
Dufour Point, 54c
Dufour, General, 30, 31
Dunant, Henry, 35, 121c

E

Edict of Nantes, 27
Eiger, the, 2d, 8c, 53, 67, 71c
Einsiedeln, 64
Einstein, Albert, 83, 84c
Emmental, 64
Engadin, 53, 54c, 59, 59c, 73c
Ensinger, Matthäus, 83c
Erasmus of Rotterdam, 24, 24c, 87, 90c
Escher, Alfred, 93c, 95
Euler, Leonhard, 27, 27c, 88
Europe, 8, 24, 30, 39, 39c, 40, 43, 43c,
    64, 67, 88c, 92c, 97c, 118, 127 (see
    also European Union)
European Economic Zone, 39, 39c
European Union, 8, 39, 39c (see also
    Europe)

F

Farmers' War, the, 27
Federal Polytechnic Institute, Zurich, 32
Fête-Dieu, 131
Feuchtmayer, Joseph Anton, 98c
First World War, 36, 36c
Flanders, 104
Flue, St. Nicholas of, 22, 23c
Föhn, wind, 51
Formazza, 113
Forn Pass, 59
France, 18, 24, 25, 27, 28c, 30, 31, 37,
    64, 67, 88c, 118, 127
Francis I of France, 22, 22c
Frauenfeld, 74
Frederick II of Hohenstaufen, 20, 31
Fribourg Canton, 124, 133c
Fribourg, 18, 20, 22, 24, 30, 74, 76, 77,
    78c, 79, 104, 110-111, 131
Fuorn Cantons, Lake of the, 21, 46, 64c,
    72, 73c, 104, 106c (see also Lucerne,
    Lake)
Furka Pass, 54c, 67, 73c
Fürst, Walter, 20c, 21

G

Gallen, St., 18, 98
Gansabhauet Festival, 127, 127c
Gaul, 18
Geigy, 87
Geissler, Christian, 27c
Generoso, Mt., 72
Geneva, 24, 24c, 27c, 30, 35, 35c, 36,
    39, 39c, 67, 69c, 74, 77, 114, 114c,
    118-121, 131
Geneva, Lake, 2c, 18, 46, 46c, 118c
Germany, 20, 32, 46, 64, 64c, 65c, 88c,
    131
Gessler, bailiff, 21
Giacometti, Alberto, 95, 95c
Gianadda Foundation, 113
Giornico, battle of, 22
Girard-Perregaux, chronometer, 8c
Giron, Charles, 84c
Glarus Canton, 24, 51, 127
Glarus, 124c
Glass building, 121c
God's House, the League of, 109
Gornergletscher Glacier, 43c

Göschenen, 72
Gotthardbahn, 95
Grand Combin, Mt., 53, 53c
Grandson, battle of, 22
Great St. Bernard Hostel, 54c
Great St. Bernard Pass, 18, 20, 53, 67,
    69, 113
Gregory X, pope, 8c, 114
Grey League, the, 109
Grindelwald, 67, 71c
Grisons Canton, 18, 24, 25, 29, 40, 43,
    46, 53, 62c, 73c, 109, 124, 127
Grütli, 35
Gruyère, 64, 110, 128
Guisan, General Henri, 37

H

Hackert, Carl, 2c
Hallstatt, 18c
Hapsburg, dinasty, 20, 21, 74, 88, 104
Helvetia, 18, 20, 110
Helvetian Society, 27
Helvetic Republic, 21, 22, 27c, 28, 29,
    109, 127
Herbstfastnacht, 131
Hérens, 67
Hérens, bovine breed, 129, 129c
Hesse, Herman, 123
History Museum, Bern, 18c
Hodler, Ferdinand, 83, 95
Holbein, 88c
Holland, 27
Hölloch Cave, 51
Holy Alliance, 30
Holy Roman Empire, 20, 21, 109, 113
Hornuss, 133
Hospice de Beaune, 90c
Huguenots, 87

I

Inn, River, 40, 46, 54c, 59
Interlaken, 67, 124c
International Monetary Fund, 39
International Red Cross, 35, 35c, 39
Italy, 8c, 22, 27, 32, 36, 37, 39, 53, 54c,
    67, 72, 104

J

Jeanneret, Charles Edouard (known as
    Le Corbusier), 103
Jean-Richard, Daniel, 103
Jenatsch, Jörg, 25
Julia Equestris, 18 (see also Nyon)
Julier Pass, 53, 54c
Julius Caesar, 18
Jungfrau Massif, 2c, 8, 50c, 53, 67, 71c
Jungfraujoch, 71c
Junod, Charles-Henri, 103
Jura, 18, 20, 32, 40, 43, 46, 64, 74, 79,
    103

K

Kappel, War of, 24
Klausen Pass, 8c
Klee, Paul, 83
Kleine Scheidegg, 50c
Klimsenhorn Chapel, 64c
Knox, John, 24c, 120c, 121
Kyburg, dynasty, 20, 74

L

La Chaux-de-Fonds, 8c, 102-103
Landsgemeinde, 124c, 127
LaRoche, 88
Lausanne, 28, 31, 32c, 67, 69c, 74,
    114-117
Lavater, 95
Le Locle, 103

League of the Confederates, 90c
League of the Swiss Cantons, 92
League of the Ten Jurisdictions, 109
League of the Thirteen Cantons, 21
Léman, Lake, 18, 24c, 40, 46, 67, 69c,
  74, 77c, 114, 114c, 118, 118c, 119c
  (see also Geneva, Lake)
Lemanic Republic, 28
Lenzburg, 74
Lenzerheide, 109
Leopold III of Austria, 21
Lepontians, 18
Leukerbad, 40
Limmat River, 46, 92, 92c, 95, 95c
Lindau Psalm Book, 18c
Lindenhof, 92
Linth-Limmat, River, 46
Linth, River, 43
Locarno, 22
Locarno, Lake, 46, 72 (see also
  Maggiore, Lake)
Loetschental, 131
Lombardy, 30, 104, 109
Lötschen, River, 40c, 131c
Louis XVI, 104
Lucerne Canton, 64c, 127c
Lucerne, 20, 24, 64c, 74, 74c, 76, 77,
  77c, 104-107, 124c, 127, 131
Lucerne, Lake, 46, 72, 73c (see also
  Four Cantons, Lake of)
Ludwig the German, 95c
Lugano, 22, 74, 121d, 123, 131
Lugano, Lake, 46, 46c, 72, 72c, 122c
  (see also Ceresio, Lake)
Luini, Bernardino, 123, 123c
Lukmanier Pass, 20, 53, 76c, 109
Luther, Martin, 24

M
Maggia, River, 46
Maggiore, Lake, 46, 72 (see also
  Locarno, Lake)
Maloja Pass, 59
Marignano, battle of, 22, 22c
Martigny, 18, 69c, 113 (see also
  Octodurus)
Massena, André, 28c
Matterhorn, the, 53
Matterhorn, the, 8, 8c, 53, 53c, 67, 71c
Mazzini, Giuseppe, 30
Mediterranean Sea, 40, 46
Meglinger, Kaspar, 106c
Mendrisio, 22
Mesolcina Valley, 109
Milan, 22, 28, 123
Mme. de Staël, 118
Molèson, 64
Mönch, the, 2c, 8c, 53, 67, 71c
Mont Blanc, 2c, 54c
Mont Pélérin, 67
Montagnola, 123
Monte Rosa, 43c, 53, 53c, 54c, 71c
Montreux, 67
Morat, 20, 74, 76, 79
Morat, battle of, 22
Morat, Lake, 46
Morgarten, battle of, 21
Morges, 74
Morteratsch Glacier, 43, 59, 59c
Moser, Karl, 95
Motta, Giuseppe, 36
Mummentschanz, 131
Muota, 51, 128
Mussolini, Benito, 36
Mustair Valley, 59
Mythen, 72, 84c

N
Näfels, battle of, 21
Nancy, battle of, 22
Nestlé, 110
Neuchâtel, 30, 32, 103, 131

Neuchâtel, Lake, 46
New York, 121c
Nicolao, Saint, 131 (see also
  Samichlaus)
Nidwald Canton, 127
North Sea, 40, 46, 64c
Northeast Railway, 95
Notre-Dame Cathedral, Lausanne, 8c
Novartis, 87
Novena Pass, 67
Novena-Furka-Grimsel-Susten Pass, 53
Nyon, 18

O
Oberaletsch Glacier, 43
Oberalp, 73c
Obergabelhorn, Mt., 53c
Oberland, Bernese, 8c, 43c, 46c, 128
Obwald Canton, 22, 73c, 127
Octodurus, 18, 69c, 113 (see also
  Martigny)
Orbe, River, 51
Orchestra of the Swiss Romande, 114
Oscar Reinhart Museum, 95
Ossola, 113
Otmar, St., 98

P
Paris, 28, 30
Pavia, 22c
Peace of Aarau, 27
Perret-Gentil, 103
Pestalozzi, Ioahnn Heinrich, pedagogue,
  27, 95
Petite Arvine, 69c
Phyton Georges, 110
Piaget, Jean, 121
Piano, Renzo, 83
Pilatus, Mt., 43, 64, 64c, 72, 73c, 106
Pioda, Giovan Battista, 32
Piz Bernina, mountain, 53, 54c, 59
Piz Corvatsch, mountain, 59, 59c
Piz Medel, mountain, 53c
Piz Murtel, mountain, 59
Plaine Morte Glacier, 43c
Po, River, 8, 40, 46
Po valley plain, 54c, 72
Pontresina, 59c
Porrentruy, 74
Portugal, 39
Poschiavo valley, 109
Prealps, 40, 46, 64, 72
Proust, Marcel, 46
Provence, 20
Prussia, 31

R
Raetia Prima, 109
Ramuz, Charles Ferdinand, 113
Randa, 71c
Ranft, hermit, 23c
Raron, 71c
Rentenansalt Insurance Agency, 32
Reuss, River, 43, 46, 54c, 72, 72c, 73c,
  104, 104c, 106c
Rhaetians, 18
Rheinfelden, 43
Rhine, River, 8, 18, 28c, 40, 43, 46, 48,
  53, 64, 64, 73c, 77, 86c, 87, 88, 91c,
  109
Rhone, River, 8, 18, 40, 43, 46, 54c, 67,
  67c, 69c, 71c, 74, 113, 113c, 118,
  119c
Riviera, 22
Roman Museum, Nyon, 18c
Rome, 32
Romont, 74
Roseg, Mount, 59c
Rossini, Gioacchino, 21
Rothenthurm, 64
Rousseau, Jean-Jacques, 27, 27c, 118
Rudolf I of Hapsburg, 8c, 20, 104, 114

Rudolf III, 113
Rütli, 21, 72, 84c

S
Saas Fee, valley, 71c
Saas Grund, valley, 71c
Sainte-Beuve, Charles, 114
Saint-Saphorin, 69c
Samichlaus, 131 (see also Nicolao, Saint)
San Giorgio, Mt., 72
San Salvatore, Mt., 72
Santa Maria degli Angeli, church, 123
Säntis, the, 43, 64
Sarine, River, 18, 46, 74, 76, 110, 124
Savoy Family, 20, 74, 77c
Savoy, region, 20
Schaffhausen, 22, 24, 28, 51c, 64, 64c, 76,
  133
Schiller, Friedrich, 21
Schöllenen Gorge, 43, 72
Schwingen, 132c, 133c
Schwyz Canton, 20, 21, 24, 30, 31, 51,
  72, 73c, 104, 127
Scuol, 59c
Sechseläuten, festival, 127, 127c
Second World War, 36, 37
Sedunum, 113 (see also Sion)
Sempach, battle of, 21, 104
Sforza family, 76
Sforza, Ludovic "the Moor", 22
Sforza, Maximilian, 22
Sihl, River, 46
Sils Lake, 59
Silvaplana Lake, 59, 59c
Simplon Pass, 32, 32c, 54c, 67, 71c
Sion, 113, 113c (see also Sedunum)
Sluperius, Jean, 22c
Society of Nations, 36
Soletta, 20, 22, 24, 27
Solferino, battle of, 35, 35c
Sonderbund, 30, 106
Spain, 24, 25, 39
Spalen, 88
Spiez, 46c
Splügen Pass, 20, 53
St. Bernard Pass, 53
St. Gallen, 2c, 20, 22, 29, 32, 74, 98-
  101
St. Gotthard Pass, 8c, 20, 22, 28c, 32,
  32c, 43, 50c, 53, 54c, 72, 73c, 74c,
  76c, 93c, 95, 104, 106c
St. Margrethen Pass, 36c
St. Martin, church, 108c
St. Maurice, 18
St. Moritz, 59, 59c, 109
St. Moritz, Lake, 59
St. Niklaus, 71c
St. Ursanne, 74
Stans, 23c
Stauffacher, Werner, 20c, 21
Stein am Rhein, 74, 74c
Studer, Friedrich, 83
Sun King, the, Louis XIV, 26c
Sursee, 127, 127c
Suvorov, general, 28c
Suze River, 64
Swiss Labor Federation, 35
Swiss League, 79, 118
Swiss National Park, 59
Swiss Plateau, 18, 40, 43, 46, 64, 65c, 74

T
Tamaro, Mt., 123
Tarasp, castle, 59c
Täsch, 71c
Tell, William, 20c, 21, 133
Thirty Years' War, the, 24c, 25
Thun Lake, 46, 46c, 74c
Thun, 74, 76
Thurgau, 21, 22, 29
Ticino Canton, 18, 29, 30, 35, 109,
  124, 131

Ticino river, 40, 43, 46, 72
Tinguely, Jean, 88, 88c
Titlis, Mt. 72
Toggenburg, 64, 128
Tourbillon, 113c
Treaty of Versailles, 36
Treaty of Westphalia, 24c, 25
Trugberg, Mt., 8c
Tschäggättä, 131
Tuileries, the, 106
Turicum, 92
Twain, Mark, writer, 106c
Tzara, Tristan, 95

U
U.N., 118, 121c
UNESCO, 67, 71c, 76, 76c
United Nations, 39, 39c
Unspunnen Canton, 124c, 127
Unspunnen, 127
Unteraare Glacier, 43
Unterwald Canton, 21, 24, 30, 72, 73,
  104, 127
Urani, 20
Uri Canton, 8c, 20, 21, 22, 24, 30, 40,
  53, 72, 73c, 104

V
Valais Canton, 8c, 30, 40, 40c, 51, 53,
  53c, 67, 71c, 73c, 113, 113c, 124,
  129, 131, 131c
Valère, 113
Vallée de Joux, 103
Vallemaggia, 22
Vallotton, Félix, 95
Vals, 40
Valtellina, 30, 54c, 109
Vaud, 20, 22, 24, 28, 29, 30, 79, 114c
Verbier, 53c
Versailles, 26c, 28c
Vertex of Geneva, 39c
Vevey, 129c
Veveyse, 46, 69c, 77c
Viamala Gorge, 43
Villars, 67
Villars, industry, 110
Villmergen, War of, 27
Vindonissa, 18 (see also Windisch)
Visconti family, 76
Voltaire, 114, 118
Von Melchtal, Arnold, 20c, 21
Von Rheinfelden, Johannes, 133
Von Winkelried, Arnold, 20c

W
Walsers, 113, 124
Weggis, 128
Weisshorn, Mount, 53
Wetterhorn, 71c
White Lake, the, 46, 54c
Windisch, 18
Winterthur, 95
World Bank, the, 39

Y
Young Europe Association, 30c
Yverdon, 74

Z
Zähringen, 20, 110
Zähringen, Berthold V, 79
Zähringen, dukes, 74, 74c, 78c
Zermatt, 53c, 67, 71c
Zernez, 59
Zug Canton, 24 30
Zug, 74, 74c
Zug, Lake, 46
Zürich, Lake, 46
Zürich, 20, 22, 24, 27, 27c, 28, 30, 32,
  39, 46, 74, 74c, 77, 92-97, 114c,
  121c, 127, 127c
Zwingli, Ulrich, 24, 24c, 92, 95

PHOTO CREDITS

136 In Basel's Markt-platz stands the magnificent Rathaus – the Town Hall – erected in the 14th century and renovated between the 16th and 17th centuries, when the façade was decorated with charming trompe-l'oeil *panels.*